ALSO BY LEROY MCKENZIE JR.

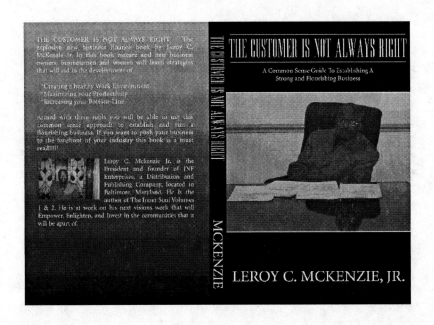

THE CUSTOMER IS NOT ALWAYS RIGHT — The explosive new business finance book by Leroy C. McKenzie Jr. In this book mature and new business owners, businessmen and women will learn strategies that will aid in the development of:

*Creating a healthy Work Environment
*Maximizing your Productivity
*Increasing your Bottom-Line

Armed with these tools you will be able to use this common sense approach to establish and run a flourishing business. If you want to push your business to the forefront of your industry this book is a must read!!!!!

Leroy C. Mckenzie Jr. is the President and founder of JNF Enterprises, a Distribution and Publishing Company, located in Baltimore, Maryland. He is the author of The Inner Soul Volumes 1 & 2. He is at work on his next visions work that will Empower, Enlighten, and Invest in the communities that it will be apart of.

THE CUSTOMER IS NOT ALWAYS RIGHT

A Common Sense Guide To Establishing A Strong and Flourishing Business

MCKENZIE

LEROY C. MCKENZIE, JR.

Young & gifted
"The New Generation Of Entrepreneurship"

By Leroy C. Mckenzie Jr.

*To Oscar,
Thanks for the love
and Support. Never
Stop Believing!!*

Leroy Jr

JNF ENTERPRISES
BALTIMORE, MARYLAND

First Published by JNF Enterprises 5/2007

Young & Gifted The New Generation of Entrepreneurship/by Leroy McKenzie.

Includes index.
ISBN 978-0-9793012-1-6

Library of Congress Control Number: 2007929348

Cover Design by Brian Harding

DEDICATION

This book is dedicated to my silent partners Melva J. McKenzie, and Sandra L. Cooper. You have been there for me through this entire journey that I am on. I cannot thank you enough for believing enough in me to support me not only with your words but in your actions. I can only hope that what I do is half as much as you have done for me. I love ya.

Leroy Jr.

Acknowledgements

I want to first thank my Lord and Savior Jesus Christ for giving me this vision. Without you Lord I am nothing. I would like to say thank you to all of the entrepreneurs that took part in this project. Thank you for believing in what you do and what I am doing. Your experience and knowledge that you share is invaluable and I hope that what you do for our communities will for ever be remembered.

I would next like to thank my family, my sisters Larissa Neal and Toussant Hart. My nieces and Nephew, Kiona, Raven, Jasmine, Little Derrick Hart Jr., and the rest of my family. I love all of you. My co-pilot Monica, thanks for the insights. My friends, Rhonique Bryant, Sheila Elliott, David Wiggins, Craig Johnson, Brian Howard, Tonya "Custom"Harris, Maurice Shines, Wendy Friend and the K&G crew. Thank you all for supporting a young business man's vision, and help to make it a reality.

Last but certainly not least, I would like to thank my Pastor Bishop Walter S. Thomas Sr. You have enlightened, empowered, and invested in me. You have taught me to go beyond what I believe and to trust God in everything that I do, and to believe It Can Be Done!

Table of contents

Forward

An entrepreneur is defined as a person who organizes, manages, and assumes responsibility for a business or other enterprise.

There are those in life who are called to lead and there are those who are called to follow. The word that sits above defines those of us who have chosen to answer the call and lead. Just as Moses chose to answer the call of the burning bush, and David received the calling of being King, we entrepreneurs of the 21st century have chosen to build our visions. What I have chosen to do in the pages that follow is to highlight some entrepreneurs who have taken the mantle that has been passed to them and to carve their names in the history of business and industry. Entrepreneurship is not something that should be entered into lightly. The task that comes with entrepreneurship is very demanding. If it were easy then everyone would be doing it.

In our society today so much emphasis is placed on the negative aspect of business. We hear, on a daily basis, the corrupt and the detrimental side of businesses today. The newspapers, radio, and television, are filled with stories of business owners who seem to have gone over to the dark side of business and industry. What would make someone in this day and time want to take on the risk of starting and having their own business when over half of businesses fail within the first five years? What makes these businessmen and women that you will meet in the next few chapters stand out from others?

So much emphasis is given to the music, sports, and entertainment industries that I wanted to show that there are many of us who do business in many other industries and are successful. There is nothing wrong with being in music, sports or entertainment, but we must understand that we can do and be so much more. We must begin to understand the importance of economic leverage in this day and time.

If we are ever to move forward in our society and communities then we must begin to change our way of thinking. There must be a paradigm shift in our mentality. In the next few pages and chapters you will meet entrepreneurs who are in different industries and have had different journey's that took them to where they are today. Their success is not measured by their profit & loss statements. Nor is their success measured by the cars they drive or the houses they live in, but their success can be measured by the visions they have fulfilled and the calling that they have chosen to answer.

These "Young & Gifted" individuals have become a part of an exclusive club that not too many want to take the risk and be privy to. They have chosen to be a part of the doing generation and not the talking generation. Their legacies will be memorable and will be a part of our society for what we hope will be years to come. In highlighting this "New Generation" I hope that they will show that the way we do business in the new age is impactful, inspiring and provocative.

Each and every one of these entrepreneurs has imparted to me something that will forever stay with me. They have given me their backgrounds, insights, and experiences, that I hope to shared with you. Their stories are one that I felt should be told and shared with others so that we can begin to change our way of thinking. Welcome to the 21st century way of entrepreneurship. This is the way we do it!! Meet the **"Young & Gifted, The New Generation of Entrepreneurs"!!**

Chapter 1
The Queen of Triple Crown

VICKIE STRINGER

CEO
TRIPLE CROWN PUBLICATIONS

INTRODUCTION

Triple Crown Publications began in 2001 with the self-publishing of author Vickie Stringer's book "Let That Be The Reason". The letters T.C.P. have history and significant meaning for the author. During her past life in crime it was always said that in the streets "one should stay down for their crown". With desire, drive, and determination to give up her life of crime, she once again decided to "stay down for her crown". Once running with a crew called the "Triple Crown Posse", the author started her own publishing company and named it Triple Crown Publications. This company is continuing to introduce an amazing stable of talented, emerging authors.

Ms. Stringer has also written two other novels, "Imagine This", and Dirty Red, and written the self-publishing instructional guide, "How To Succeed In the Publishing Game". Public speaking, motivational seminars, and mentoring programs are also a large part of her busy schedule. "I use my life as an example to warn others of the danger of the drug game". The vision for the company is longevity, integrity, gripping unforgettable tales, and prosperity.

In April of 2004, I picked up the current issue of Black Issues Magazine. As I flipped through the magazine reading the different articles, one particular article stuck out the most to me. The article was about a young woman, who was an up and coming author and entrepreneur. The article caught my attention because of the story that this amazing woman had to tell. The article talked about a woman who was a part of the "drug game", completely turned her life around and has become one of the foremost entrepreneurs in the publishing industry.

In November of that same year, the Black Writers Guild of Maryland Prince Georges chapter, of which I was the Executive Director for two years, had an author by the name of Vickie Stringer, coming to speak for one of our monthly meetings. When I saw the name initially, I did not recognize it as the same name of the woman from the article that I had read.

Then as I started to read the author's bio I recognized her from the article that I had read several months before. When I realized that they were one in the same, I got excited about the opportunity to meet this woman. When I had the opportunity to not only meet her but to introduce her, I was even more excited. When we had the opportunity to talk after the meeting and during the drive to drop her off at the airport, I became even more impressed in what this young woman had to say.

Ms. Stringer is not only beautiful but she is someone that will capture you with her passion and drive for what she does. Ms. Stringer has a genuiness that not many of her stature possess. She is not only modest but humble, and success is the only option in everything that she does. When I read her first and second novels about her life I was even more of a Vickie Stringer fan. Her journey to entrepreneurship has not been an easy one but it is easy to see why this woman is as successful as she is and will be for a long time.

When I first started developing my list of entrepreneurs for this book she was the first one that I thought of. Ms. Stringer is what defines entrepreneurship. Her vision has never wavered and she is an inspiration to anyone who she comes in contact with. She is someone that will capture your heart, and leave you with words that encourage your soul. She is a mother first, entrepreneur second, and business woman last. She has created a brand and name that will last forever. She is who I call "The Queen Of Triple Crown", and she wears her crown well. Meet Ms. Vickie Stringer of **Triple Crown Publications.**

<u>BEGINNINGS</u>

As a young girl growing up in East Detroit, Ms. Stringer attended Cass Tech, which is one of the top schools in the Detroit school system. She is one of seven children born to her parents, who were both hard working individuals. After high school, she entered Western Michigan University, and then entered Ohio State University. After her freshman year, Ms. Stringer decided to pursue other interests. Although she did not finish school at Ohio State University, she still believes that education is important. In speaking with Ms. Stringer, she believes that attending school is not a prerequisite for one being a successful entrepreneur. She has definitely proven that success is not given to anyone, but earned by those who pursue it.

Ms. Stringer started Triple Crown in December of 2001. Little did she know that her experiences up to that point would be the very foundation of her now flourishing publishing company. Ms. Stringer has no problem speaking about her past and how her life has changed since she spent time in a Federal Prison. She uses her life as a living example to show that "God is a Restorer", says Ms. Stringer. One only has to read her story and to talk with her to know that this young entrepreneur was destined for success. Her strong work ethic and charming personality have been what has built Triple Crown into the premier publishing company of Hip-Hop fiction.

In 2001, a young lady, started a company on hope. Ms. Stringer took what was deep in her soul and began on a journey that would lead her to the top of the publishing industry. None of us knows what God has in store for us. We all go through trials and tribulations and we sometimes wonder why God has us go through these things. Our experiences are ours individually and when we go through those situations, we don't always understand why, but when we reflect back on those experiences we realize that we may not be where we are had we not gone through those experiences.

This is true for Ms. Stringer as well. She journalized her first novel, which was a testament to her life and experiences. Little did she know that those experiences would be the vehicle used to lift her into a prolific writer and entrepreneur. Ms. Stringer started by selling her books out of the trunk of her car and soon found that her story was one that would capture and provide inspiration to many people. As Ms. Stringer told me, "Triple Crown was started on hope". That hope was the foundation that has kept Triple Crown Publications going since the beginning.

After selling her books and seeing the impact that they had on others she gained instant success.

After the success of her first, novel Ms. Stringer has grown her company from being run out of her home to being run in a business district in the outskirts of Columbus, Ohio. As I pulled up to the office building, in the quiet area, not far from the Columbus Airport, I soon walked into the world known as Triple Crown Publications. Ms. Stringer employ's nine individuals, who she considers family. As I was greeted by her assistant, I soon came to feel the family type atmosphere that surrounded me.

As I spent my morning with Ms. Stringer, it was easy to see why she has been the successful businesswoman that she is. Her warm spirit and encompassing smile would make any person feel right at home as she spoke with them. As we talked she would make me feel right at home while she multi-tasked in her office. Her love and passion for Triple Crown was evident as she came to greet me. She excitedly showed me the current issue of Essence Magazine, which had just done an article on her and her business. Since the beginning of Triple Crown, Ms. Stringer has been in numerous magazines and received awards for her writing.

Triple Crown Publications distributes over one million books to bookstores and libraries throughout the United States and abroad. Ms. Stringer makes no qualms about publishing strictly hip-hop/urban fiction. Believing in the niche that she has carved for Triple Crown, she has opened the door for other authors to have their stories heard. Just as she has given individuals a chance for employment, who otherwise may not have been given a chance. She has given authors a chance, who might not have been signed by traditional and mainstream publishing companies. Triple Crown has awakened a voice in the publishing industry that has totally been ignored. With that voice, Triple Crown has produced some of the most griping urban fiction that is written today.

Starting and keeping Triple Crown in the forefront of the publishing industry has not been easy. Ms. Stringer believes that nothing comes easy. It takes hard work and dedication to stick with your dream. Ms. Stringer says, "There is no easy way to success". She believes that you must go hard at it every single day. From the beginning of Triple Crown Ms. Stringer has gone hard at achieving success. By befriending a graphic artist and getting the support of her friends and family, Ms. Stringer is building an empire and legacy that will go far beyond the publishing industry. Setting out to change the face of the publishing industry, she has broken down the doors of the publishing industry and created her own lane in a male dominated industry.

Triple Crown has gone from publishing one author to now having over 30 authors on its roster. From the bookstores to the libraries, Triple Crown Publications is becoming one of the major players in the publishing game. With its new hip-hop flava Triple Crown and its Queen (Stringer), will no doubt have readers anxiously awaiting their next novel. With her market clearly defined Ms. Stringer has Triple Crown headed in the right direction.

Ms. Stringer has it on a course that will lead it to greater heights and many exciting filled days. Ms. Stringer had hopes of having an impact in the communities and that her books would be a part of those communities. They have done that and so much more. As the company continues to grow it will begin to have an even greater impact by uplifting and enlightening her target audience. The road to success is filled with many bumps but it seems as if Ms. Stringer and Triple Crown are handling that road with enthusiasm and confidence.

THE INDUSTRY

A few years ago, my friend and I went to see the movie "The Gospel". As we watched the telling tale of a young man struggling with his spirituality and family, I leaned over to her and asked her "did you ever think that 5 or 10 years ago we would be in a theatre watching a movie about God". She promptly responded "no". Just as my friend and I never fathomed the idea of being in a movie theatre watching a movie that glorified God, the same can be said for Ms. Stringer and Triple Crown Publications. When she first started out not even 5 years ago in the publishing industry Hip-Hop and Urban Fiction was not even heard of. Since that time she has opened the doors and eyes of the publishing industry to a completely new genre of literature.

For years the publishing industry has been pigeon holed to what it has believed was their formula for what works. Well, as with the music industry the publishing industry is finding out that we in Black America have the ability to change the face of any industry that we choose to become a part of. Ms. Stringer has taken the publishing industry doors and broken through them like no one has ever done before. Publishing is a very hard industry to break into, just as any other industry, but Ms. Stringer has found her niche in this male dominated field and staked her claim as one of the industries foremost publishers and writers.

As I reflect back over the publishing industry, as I did the movie industry, that warm summer day in the movie theatre, I say the same thing now about the strides that have been made to put the publishing industry on notice, that you can no longer use traditional means to reach target markets that were once believed to be unreachable or that were not even considered more than five years ago. Ms. Stringer and Triple Crown have changed the way that bookstores look at African American writers and the value that they bring to the market. One of the key elements of any great CEO and company is its ability to have name recognition. Triple Crown Publications is moving fast to the forefront of the publishing industry because of its ground-breaking authors and the stick-to-itiveness of its visionary leader.

Ms. Stringer has believed in the stories that are being told by her authors and the voice that she is giving them. She believes in giving those who might not have been given a second thought by mainstream publishing houses a chance to sound their trumpets and be acknowledged for the piece of the publishing industry pie that they have carved out for themselves and Triple Crown. It is not an easy thing to stay true to something when others in an industry tell you that no one will want to read that or no one will buy those types of books. Ms. Stringer took those rejections she received when she first started out in the industry and parleyed them into the motivation to not only create her own company but to take what she learned from her experiences and give others the opportunity that she was not given.

As any writer will tell you it is very difficult to break into the publishing industry. Industry executives of yesterday will soon find themselves a long forgotten entity if they do not find the ability to see the changing times that are occurring by the day in the publishing industry. Technology is making the industry extremely leveled with the increased improvements to the internet, publishing avenues, and the ability of authors to go the independent route if they choose.

The publishing industry is going through a paradigm shift and that shift is being created by Ms. Stringer and Triple Crown. To be an entrepreneur you have to have very tough skin because there will be many who do not see what you see. They will not get what you get or feel what you feel. In spite of the fears that come with any venture we must push forward in our perspective industries. We can't worry about what others will think if we do this or if we don't do that. What matters most is what God thinks and what we think.

The publishing industry is filled with giants, some who take authors and use them as bottom-line dollar signs, but amongst the giants, is a family oriented company, started by a woman who has not been ashamed to talk about where she has come from and lifted not only herself but a number of others who have chosen to follow her lead. Triple Crown Publications may not be a mainstream publishing house yet, but it is becoming the place that you want to be if you want to get your voice heard in the Hip-Hop literature world.

It is rare that you encounter companies and people that make you feel as if you are family from the first time that you meet them. I experienced that warm and family type of feeling and atmosphere when I visited Triple Crown Publications. The closeness that you get stems from the top on down and can be felt all throughout the company. Mainstream publishing houses could take a page from Triple Crown's notebook on having a positive impact on the industry and how to treat your customers.

Ms. Stringer's belief is that customer service is the backbone of any industry. Believing if you work very hard you will be successful is her mantra. Her customers have made Triple Crown what it is today. Helping her customers to understand that street life is not the way to go is the purpose of Ms. Stringer and Triple Crown. When a Triple Crown reader buys one of its books they will be getting something that will enlighten them to what the "Life" is all about and the ways of the street. Is the publishing industry ready for the "Realness" that Triple Crown brings? Well, the answer so far has been a resounding Yes!

THE FUTURE

As I sat in the lobby of Triple Crown Publications I glanced through some of the magazines and books that sat on the table in front of me. I had the chance to read a couple of the articles that had been written on Ms. Stringer. As I finished one article and placed the paper back on the table, I noticed a book by Triple Crown that had been translated into another language. This intrigued me because it was the first time that I had seen something like this.

My mind quickly started racing and thinking how Triple Crown has a fan base that reaches globally. When I talked with Ms. Stringer about where she sees Triple Crown Publications going in the future and how this globalization of Triple Crown occurred, she smiled and said that the success of her books caught on abroad and has been growing ever since. Hip-Hop Literature is truly here to stay.

The success of her books abroad truly shows that the ingredients for a good book is its content because if the content is good then it can reach readers anywhere. Just as Hip-hop music has become a mainstay in our society, Hip-Hop literature is quickly becoming one as well. When asked where Triple Crown goes from here, Ms. Stringer simply says, "Wherever God takes us". With her strong faith in God and believing in where he is taking her and her company, Triple Crown has the foundation to maintain its strong hold on the publishing industry.

In this modern era it is important to have a presence both nationally and internationally. The advancements that are being made in technology are making it possible for companies such as Triple Crown to have a piece of the global market. This can only help make Triple Crown an even stronger company financially. Companies must be able to see beyond the unreachable in order to be able to grow and go further. Ms. Stringer has done this with Triple Crown Publications, by opening her company up to the global market and building a new market for herself and Triple Crown. I believe a company must always be looking for new markets to delve into. It is one way for a company to increase its bottom line. By exposing Triple Crown to the global market Ms. Stringer is also introducing her new market to something that they might not otherwise be introduced to. Mainstream publishing houses would not even think to introduce this type of genre to the global market several years ago, but now their eyes are wide open to the fact of the impact that Hip-Hop Literature has on the global market.

In order for a company to be able to move into the future, I believe there has to be a certain amount of diversity with that company. Diversity allows a company to have different dynamics to its existence. When I say diversity I mean the types of products and services that it may offer. Ms. Stringer along with Triple Crown is a company that is looking to be progressive in its movement into the future. Having her readers be able to see her books on the screen is something that Ms. Stringer hopes to offer to them in the future.

Ms. Stringer is also a believer in giving back. She does not hesitate to help others, who were like her, and wanted to break into the publishing industry or wanted to write a book. As you can see Ms. Stringer and the Triple Crown Family are moving into the future full speed ahead. With all of the achievements that Ms. Stringer has achieved thus far there is no doubt in my mind that there are many more to come. Her street smarts along with her natural born entrepreneurial gift have taken this "Queen of Triple Crown" a long way and will no doubt take her even further in the many years to come.

THE TRIPLE CROWN FAMILY
AUTHOR'S

A.J. Rivers
Danielle Santiago
Darrell J. DeBrew
Darrell King
Deborah Mayer
Deja King
Jason Poole
Joylynn Jossel
Kane & Abel
Kashamba Williams
Keisha Ervin
Kwan
Victor L. Martin
Tu-Shonda Whitaker

Leo Sullivan
Lisa Lennox
Mallori McNeal
Nikki Turner
Quentin Carter
T. Styles
T.N. Baker
Tanika Lynch
Tracy Brown
Trustice Gentles
Vickie Stringer

CHAPTER 2
THE JOI OF COMMUNICATION

JOI THOMAS

CEO
JOIFUL COMMUNICATIONS

INTRODUCTION

Delightful, outspoken, humorous, and warm-hearted are just a few words to describe Ms. Joi Thomas. Her infectious spirit lights up a room. She is a natural born leader, and this is seen in every aspect of her life.

Ms. Thomas has been a staff member at New Psalmist Baptist Church, Baltimore, MD since July 2001. She currently works in the Media Relations and Promotions department. Her responsibilities include producing and hosting the nationally televised broadcast, doing voice overs for commercials, promotions, media planning and buying, website development, editor and chief of Empowering Disciples Magazine and keeping the image of New Psalmist and its pastor, Bishop Walter S. Thomas, Sr. intact throughout the city and nation. In past years,

Ms. Thomas has worked with WBAL-TV in Baltimore, Maryland and CNN in Atlanta Georgia. Ms. Thomas received her Bachelors degree in English from Spellman College in Atlanta, Georgia, and a Post Baccalaureate Certificate in Strategic Public Relations and Communications from Towson University in Towson, Maryland. Currently, she is working on a Masters degree in Communications Science at Towson University.

Ms. Thomas is a sought after lecturer and conference speaker. She has spoken at many events on topics including team building, event planning, mentorship, and advertising. Ms. Thomas completed work on "Kingdom Conference 2005" sponsored by New Psalmist Baptist Church. For the third year in a row she served as media coordinator for the conference, which attracted over 9,000 attendees nationwide. Her responsibilities included musical artist bookings, advertising with local and national print, radio, and television media, and coordination of all on site press. The conference was such a success that we had another one in 2006.

Ms. Thomas is a true fan of Gospel music. Her love for the genre has lead her to host a weekly radio show every Sunday on WEAA 88.9 FM from 11am to 3pm. Her show is known for a variety of music selections, spotlighting new artists, and interviews of the gospel industry's leading artists. This position has given Ms. Thomas the opportunity to host several events in the Baltimore/DC metro area. Ms. Thomas is very involved the community. She is an active member of Alpha Kappa Alpha Sorority Inc., Epsilon Omega Chapter, Baltimore, MD. In her spare time, Ms. Thomas likes to read, write, spend time with loved ones and sing. Ms. Thomas played a role in the independent film "A Shepherd of Pure Heart" which was released in September 2003, and has directed, produced, and written several plays that always debut to a standing room only audience.

Every year for the past few years my church has had our annual church conference. In the conference booklet business owners of New Psalmist Baptist Church are able to take out ads in the conference booklet to advertise their businesses. This is a great way to be able to get your business out to fellow church members as well as the many others who are a part of our conference every year. Over a year ago I picked up the conference guide and I was flipping through the pages and taking a look at the different businesses that had chosen to take advantage of the exposure they would gain through this directory.

One business that struck me was a pink and white business card that had the name of Ms. Joi Thomas on it. I knew the name and even new the face of this young lady, but what was not known was that she was a budding entrepreneur. So as I queried my mind to find out more about this young entrepreneur and what made her want to start her own business, I sought to find out who and what she did. I wanted to find out what Joiful Communications was all about.

New Psalmist Baptist Church is full of men and women who have taken on the leadership roles as entrepreneurs. I have been a member of New Psalmist since 1992 and have met and made many friends in our congregation. It does me proud to be able to include individuals who are a part of my Spiritual family in this collection of Young & Gifted Entrepreneurs. It pleases me to see that the next generation of entrepreneurs from my church are becoming the movers and shakers of today. Many will say that this generation of young people are a lost generation. Well, I know some young church folk who will say something different. The young entrepreneurs of New Psalmist are not content with just being average or ordinary. What we have learned is that we must see beyond ordinary and follow where God leads us. We are not content with just working for someone else. We want to create our own path and let our voices be heard as individuals and leaders. The baton may not have been passed to us but we have taken it and we intend to run with it until God says stop!

In my task to speak with members of my church who exemplified this very character that I described previously, I met a young lady who fit that description. She is talented, beautiful, intelligent, hard working, enthusiastic, driven, and most importantly God fearing. Meet the woman who puts the Joi in **Joiful Communication**, Ms. Joi Thomas.!

BEGINNINGS

Growing up in West Baltimore was where this young budding entrepreneur spent her childhood. The oldest of three children by her parents and the only girl made her special from the beginning. Being the oldest and the only girl would prove to be the foundation of this young lady standing out from the crowd and becoming a special businesswoman. Attending McDonough School would also be the beginning of Ms. Joi Thomas establishing herself as an individual.

Being the first African-American female in her class she would soon find it necessary to prove herself at a very young age. Learning from those experiences and progressing forward Ms. Thomas would start a Big Brothers Big Sisters Program at her school. A program she says she started to help young African-Americans who attended McDonough to know that if they needed something that they had someone and somewhere they could go. This program still continues at McDonough today. Ms. Thomas graduated from McDonough and entered Spellman

College. She graduated from Spellman College with a degree in English and she also received a Post Baccalaureate Certificate in Strategic Public Relations (PR). As you can see education plays a very important part of Ms. Thomas' life and is very important to her.

Once she graduated from Spellman she returned home and began to hone her PR skills with her home church. As she told me she thought that she liked doing things in front of the camera but soon found out that once she learned the art of PR she loved it and loved working behind the scenes and production work. She also has a love for writing, which helped to start her on the path to entrepreneurship. Along with her love for writing Ms. Thomas also has taken on the task of directing the Young Adult Choir as well as being the Director and Producer of plays at the church.

She is currently finishing her Masters Degree in Communications Management at Towson University. If you are riding in your car or at home listening to your radio on Sunday morning between the hours of 11am and 3pm, you can catch sister Joi Thomas on WEAA 88.9 FM for their Sunday morning Gospel show.

She is multi-talented and shows off her communications skills each Sunday morning during those hours. For those who think that public speaking is an easy thing or hosting a radio program is an easy thing then just ask Ms. Thomas what it takes to not only run a successful business but also host a weekly radio program. I know every Sunday when I am on my way home from church; I am always tuned to 88.9 FM to hear sister Joi and the spirit-filled music that she brings across the airways. Her background with the church and radio stations brought her into contact with others who recognized the talent and skill that she possessed and became the backdrop for her starting what is now Joiful Communications.

THE INDUSTRY

PR is the link between the media and its celebrity driven individuals and companies. We see the impact that PR has on this country from our Government to the number of companies that are in print everyday in the newspapers and on the daily news. A good PR firm can mean the elevation of your company or the demise of your business. When you have a good PR firm behind you it can mean the world to a business.

It can take a good company and make it great and make a great company even better. What most PR firms can or will give you are: press kit development, publicity campaigns, newsletters, product launches, advertisements, event photography, web designs, and trade show setups. When a company is looking for a good PR firm to do business with, they need to do their research and see how that PR firm has performed in the past.

When you are looking for a PR firm you want to do business with a firm that provides the services you need and that you are compatible with. You must match your vision for your company with where the PR firm wants to take you. The PR firm should always have your best interest at heart. As a company you should be looking to positively place your company in the media at every given opportunity.

Your PR firm should be continuously trying to get your name out there as much as possible and as often as possible. The more that people hear your name the more they will become familiar with who you are and what you do. There are many PR firms in the public relations industry. What will distinguish those great firms from the good firms are research and character. The great PR firms do their research on the companies that they will be providing services for. They take the time to get to know the companies that they will represent and the people they represent. They will also put their character and your character before profits and bottom-lines.

In 2004 Ms. Thomas believed that there was a need for a PR firm that could create the images of churches, actors and actresses, and musicians. Before starting Joiful Communications, Ms. Thomas was already doing the groundwork for her PR firm. By working with other churches both in and out of the city, she consulted with them on building their PR teams for their churches. She showed them how to design the right message for the media. As we know in this day and time the church is under much scrutiny so the right message is essential to the body of Christ. As she began talking with the different churches she soon realized that she had something special. She loved the Lord and loved doing public relations, and has figured a way to combine the two. There is nothing greater than doing what one loves to do and being able to turn that love into a business.

The PR industry is filled with companies that will take your money and do nothing for you, but Joiful Communications is a full PR firm that will have your best interest at heart. What makes them unique is their ability to tailor make anything that their clients will need. You will personally meet Ms. Thomas and not have to deal with associates or other employees. It is rare in this day and time to be able to get to meet directly with CEO/Presidents of companies unless you are a client bringing in a certain amount of money to a firm. Many companies today have lost that personal touch that is needed in order to sustain strong business relationships. With Joiful Communications it does not matter what level of client you are, you will deal directly with who is in charge and who will be making all the decisions. The thing that Ms. Thomas and Joiful Communications also bring to the table and is what will make them stand head and shoulders far above the rest is the niche that she is carving in the PR industry. The Gospel Industry is experiencing a great explosion when it comes to artist and music and these are just two of the types of clients that Joiful Communications handles.

There are not many in the PR industry that have the experience that Ms. Thomas brings to the table. She has a combination of education and practical experience, which gives her the knowledge not everyone in her industry possesses. They may have the education, which will take them to a certain point but Ms. Thomas has the knowledge of the church and the honorable spirit to back it up.

Not everyone can be honorable when it comes to business but with JoiFul Communications you have an owner who loves the Lord and puts him first in her business and with her clients. Most PR firms do not know much about the church and how they should be marketed. Ms. Thomas has positioned JoiFul Communications to not only cater to the church market but also to the secular market in what they do. This will enable her to successfully build a stronghold in the gospel market as well as the secular market. No matter what industry you are in you must diversify. The more diverse your market is the stronger your financial standing will be.

Building a strong company with a strong foundation is what Ms. Thomas is all about. Believing that any great entrepreneur must first understand that leadership is "nothing more than serving others. Being a leader does not mean that you are better than anyone it just means you have been chosen to be a forerunner to those who will follow you."

Those who have chosen to let JoiFul Communications lead their PR campaign have found that their commander will take them to levels that they never thought they might be able to reach. Believing in the vision of JoiFul Communications is what has led Ms. Thomas and her list of clients to heights unseen so far and will no doubt take them to places even further in the future. Ms. Thomas also believes that a leader should leave those who come under them better off then when they first met you. Taking this type of approach with JoiFul Communications, it is no doubt that her employees as well as her clients will be better for the experience that they will get by being with her company.

Ms. Thomas is not one of those entrepreneurs who is all about self. She believes that once you have established yourself as an entrepreneur, "you have a responsibility to go back and help someone else". "Whether it is in the community or in the church". With her busy schedule Ms. Thomas still finds time to talk with young girls who want to know all about who she is and what she does. As any entrepreneur will tell you, your time is valuable to you, so taking time out to talk with the ones who will come behind you is time well spent. Ms. Thomas believes that if she does not talk with them then who will. So many of our youth today are missing those who will sit down and talk with them. They will not learn about the many different industries and companies that we run if we do not take the time to tell them and show them what it means to be an entrepreneur.

The PR Industry is full of entrepreneurs who have made their way to the top of the industry. What is lacking are those who have taken the young PR entrepreneurs under their wings and showed them how to be successful. I am impressed when I see entrepreneurs who did not have anyone to show them how to get where they are and do what they do. Those entrepreneurs like Ms. Thomas have taken on the challenge of using the knowledge that she learned on her own, to hone her skills and I firmly believe has and will bring others along that will follow in her footsteps.

In order to be in the PR industry Ms. Thomas had to do her homework. She has studied her industry and has taken the time to learn who the movers and shakers are in the industry. She has learned who her competitors are and what they are doing. She does this not just because she is a savvy businesswoman, but also because she believes that in order to be a successful entrepreneur one has to know their industry and what everyone is doing in that industry and figure out how you can be different.

She believes that you have to distinguish yourself from others in your industry and the way that you do that is by studying them. "Knowing your industry is just one aspect of standing out amongst your industry peers", says Ms. Thomas. She is a believer in education and is always learning. Whether it is a class, conference or seminar, she believes that you should always keep abreast of what is happening in your industry. She says "if you don't keep up then you will find yourself obsolete". Well obsolete is something that is not in the future for JoiFul Communications because it and its budding entrepreneur have the tools necessary to be around for a long time.

THE FUTURE

History teaches us two things. Those things we should do and those things that we shouldn't do. In order to be a progressive company and to move into the future you must first know who you are and where you come from. Our past gives us the foundation in which to build our future on.

JoiFul communications has entered its building stage and is on that upward climb to success. Its star is shining bright and looks only to get brighter. JoiFul Communications has prepared itself to move into the PR future with its clientele and the diversity of its portfolio. Not only does Joiful Communications look to do PR for its clients but it also does writing and producing.

I remember going to the Easter Production of my church this one year. The title was "Just For Me." As I watched the production, which was written and produced by Ms. Thomas, I sat and thought to myself "what a talent this young entrepreneur is". The production was wonderfully put together and beautifully written. The production had a great combination of music, drama, and a spiritual message. It will not be long from now that hopefully we will see more productions like this coming from Ms. Thomas and JoiFul Communications.

I know if everyone enjoyed this production as much as I did then they will be thoroughly pleased with any other works that will come from what God gives to Ms. Thomas. With all the growth potential that there is in the PR industry JoiFul Communications keeps itself well balanced by being able to do more than just one thing. Being diverse keeps the steady going. When certain aspects of the industry slow down, it is balanced by the other parts that are still going strong. Realizing the impact that JoiFul Communications has on its clients, as well as those who will hear about the company, will come to know what I have come to know, that this company and its founder are just beginning.

JoiFul Communications and Ms. Thomas are geared to be a part of what I call the "Doing Generation" and not the "Talking Generation". By touching people with her PR message and firm Ms. Thomas is sounding her trumpet loud and clear. She believes that in order to move from a "Talking Generation" to a "Doing Generation" you have to first begin with education. Education is the foundation of people understanding who they are and the voice that they have in this world. In order for us to create the economic leverage that we must have in any industry we must constantly be doing.

We cannot worry about what has not happened and we must begin to make things happen. When we begin to think on those lines then we can begin to affect change in this world. Ms. Thomas has carved out her piece of being a part of the "Doing Generation" with JoiFul Communications. She has proven to have a clear vision and is moving in the direction that God is taking her. Ms. Thomas is putting the PR Industry on notice and letting all other businesses know that she and JoiFul Communications are about doing business God's way!

CHAPTER 3
MS. ELITE-PHYSIQUE

TYNESE DANIELS

CEO
ELITE-PYSIQUES

INTRODUCTION

Tynese Daniels, owner of Elite Physiques Personal Training Center, is a certified personal trainer and has had a career in the personal training industry for over 9 years. She began as a competitive bodybuilder in 1997 and went on to garner the coveted Ms. Maryland Fitness title in 2001. Ms. Daniels is highly motivated and dedicated to providing her clientele with new and innovative fitness regimens. She started Elite Physiques Personal Training Center in May 2002 with the vision of providing members with a quality cross training facility, staffed with some of the areas most qualified and experienced personnel.

Ms. Daniels has a no-nonsense approach to fitness and believes that with the proper guidance and desire that anyone can reach their targeted fitness goals. Ms. Daniels attributes her success as an effective trainer to her ability to motivate and encourage others. She has helped dozens of people reach their fitness potential through a variety of training methods. She continues to share her knowledge and educate others in the areas of fitness, nutrition and general healthcare by way of her ever-growing clientele and through lectures at various speaking engagements.

America is overweight. We have become a society that is consumed with doing the least amount of labor as possible. I am not only talking about on a job but I am talking about exercise. We eat fast food on a daily basis and we rush from place to place with our busy schedules and find ourselves gaining more and more weight. It is true that as we get older our metabolism becomes slower. We do not loose weight as we did when we were younger.

We allow our kids to sit in front of the television for hours on end and some of our school systems have even taken PE or gym out of our children's curriculum. We as adults have not done any better than our children because we do not implement the right eating habits for ourselves nor do we have a regular work out schedule to keep our bodies in the best health as possible. It pains me to see on television and even when I am going through my daily routine, to see so many individuals who are overweight. For some it cannot be helped, but that is such a small number that it pails in comparison to those who are overweight and can do something about it.

For those who choose to do something about getting their bodies in shape and treating their bodies as a temple there are some options. They can do as a friend of mine did and create her own plan of action and stick to a daily meal plan. For the individual who wants some professional help and motivation and wants to sculpt there bodies into the Adonis or Nefertiti body frame, there is a place that specializes in these types of "physiques." Not everyone is ready for what a personal trainer can offer to them. To have someone that will give you discipline and direction for your body's sake will take great focus.

I happened upon a young lady who had taken her body and the bodies of others to another level. She is someone who will charm you with her pleasant demeanor and at the same time will push you to your limits when you come under her conditioning. Just when you think you can't take it any more, she will push you even further. Your body will hurt. It will feel like it has been poked, prodded and pruned. It will hurt you to even think about what your next work out will be like, but at the end of your time when you look back at yourself and see the image that has become you, you can't do anything but smile. You smile at the physique that has been made and know that it is uniquely yours. Meet the woman that specializes in fitness physiques. That woman is Ms. Tynese Daniels of **Elite-Physiques**.

BEGINNINGS

Ms. Tynese Daniels is a native of Baltimore who also grew up in the Columbia, Maryland area. She is the oldest of 3 children. She attended Howard High School in Columbia and then attended

34

Bowie State University. After growing up in a predominately white area in Howard County, Ms. Daniels went on to attend a Historically Black College and University (HBCU) at Bowie State University, which was a big difference from the area that she had grown up in. Going from an area that has very few people of color to a University that is dominated with people of your same hue can be a culture shock. Ms. Daniels and I spoke on the difference between going to a predominantly white university and going to a Historically Black University. There is something special about going to an HBCU, as anyone who has graduated or attended one will tell you. The experience that you get while there is like no other, as Ms. Daniels attested to.

While attending Bowie State University Ms. Daniels was introduced to fitness and would find out that it would be her path to entrepreneurship. She graduated from Bowie State with a degree in Marketing, which she has found to come in handy in running her own business. After leaving Bowie State, she began to continue her fitness frenzy at a local Bally's facility. As she would come in for her routine workouts, she would be befriended by a trainer who taught her the techniques of working her body. She would be intrigued by the way; that her body started to look and began to ask questions that would help her to understand her body from a fitness perspective.

As time went on she would have individuals that would ask her how she got her great body and she soon found that there were many who wanted to be able to get their bodies to look like hers. Ms. Daniels would take the opportunity of the knowledge she gained from her workout partner to become a certified fitness trainer and turn the inquiries that she got about her body into clients. Beginning with becoming a fitness trainer for Bally's she found herself wanting more. While holding down a full-time job she was able to build her clientele. With the assistance of her mentor Mr. Kenneth Banks, she was able to strengthen her personal training knowledge and at the same time supplement her income. As she told me, "it was a win/win situation". He was able to get the sales and marketing assistance that he needed and I was able to work the flexible hours that I needed in order to build my business." After her clientele had grown to the point that she was cutting back her hours with her mentor a decision had to be made. Mr. Banks came to her and said that she needed to decide what she wanted to do.

After much deliberation, she finally decided that it was time to leave the nest. Although there was some apprehension, she knew that it was something that she had to do. From that moment came Elite-Physiques.

THE INDUSTRY

The fitness industry back in the day was a very competitive industry. When she first started, Ms. Daniels talked about the difference between working for a private fitness club and a very public one. It was more competitive in the public fitness club because of the amount of business that would flow through. The private club had more of a fixed clientele so there was not much of a change or flow of clients. What she learned was that she had to find her niche in the industry and that niche was gearing her services more towards everyday workout people as opposed to the more competitive individuals. When she speaks of competitive people she is talking about those who may be in fitness competitions across the country.

With Ms. Daniels being Ms. Maryland Fitness 2001, she could see that she wanted to position herself was by being more involved with those individuals that were not in competitions. In the competitive aspect of her industry, she talked about their not being a steady flow of clients and she wanted to be consistent with getting clients in her doors. So going from competitive clients to everyday clients has made a difference for her and her business in the past few years. It has proven to be the right move for this young entrepreneur because she has found her everyday clients to be much kinder than the competitive clients .

Ever since I was a young boy, I have always been interested in the many factors that affect the flow of industries. For the fitness industry, one of the things that is having a profound affect on the industry is plastic surgery. Ms. Daniels sees plastic surgery as one of the major factors that is making it easier for people not to have to work out. She says that, "more and more people are turning to plastic surgery as opposed to loosing weight the traditional way". We live in a time where people want things done yesterday. They have adopted the microwave mentality

36

even when it comes to fitness. Plastic surgery is more affordable now days so you find individuals opting to do it rather than sweat and burn those calories off.

People feel as if they do not have the time nor do they want to make the effort to get their health in order. This fad is becoming more prevalent in the African-American community today. What we once thought was just something that Caucasians did we now have found as an option. Another issue that is also having an effect on the fitness industry is the amount of diet pills and liquid diets that you see on the market. Just as people have tried to substitute the regular workout regiment for the quick fix, they have found, as Ms. Daniels says, "they do not work".

Ms. Daniels says, "what people have to realize is that the diet pills and liquid diets do not work because they are one sided". They will help you to loose the weight but once you loose the weight and you come off the diet, you gain the weight back plus more. You gain the weight back because you go from just being on the pills back to eating regular food. Ms. Daniels says, "most people have poor eating habits". People in the past were not willing to take the risk of using diet pills or the many other diet supplements that you see commercials for, but now that people are more desperate to loose weight quickly and easily they are trying them.

These diets and diet supplements do not teach people about healthy eating habits, and as a result, people will pay the price in the future. You will find more and more unhealthy people. Ms. Daniels believes, since we do not know the long term effects of these drugs we do not know if people will have complications from them in the years to come. People have to realize that there are no short cuts to being and staying healthy. Our society wants us to think that we can have everything now and that just is not so. Anything that is worth having is worth working hard for and that includes our health. Ms. Daniels takes pride in caring about her clients. She not only wants her clients to see great results in the way that their body looks but to also understand how it got to look the way it looks and how to keep it looking that way. The more educated that we are about our health the better off we will be. People have to understand that we can still have the pizzas, subs, and burgers, but we must do it in moderation and we must exercise.

Ms. Daniels believes that both in the near and not to distant future, there will be a shift in her industry. From the many exercise machines that you see advertised on television to the different cooking apparatuses that promote healthy eating. The industry is changing but not necessarily in a good way, Ms. Daniels says, "The industry is now geared towards the quick fixes", and if people do not recognize this, Ms. Daniels believes the industry will head down the wrong road. When a client enters the doors of Elite-Physiques, they do not have to worry about going down that wrong road. They will enter a world that is focused on getting them in the best physical condition possible. This can be done because what makes Elite-Physiques unique is that you have a combined 40 years of fitness experience under one roof and you will not find that anywhere else in Baltimore. That is something that bodes well in an industry where its clients rely heavily on what you know and not who you know. The more you know about the body and the foods that you should eat the more confident you will feel about the trainer that is getting your body into shape. If I am sweating and can't eat the foods that I want to then I want to know that the person who is training me knows what they are talking about, and at Elite-Physiques, they know what they are talking about.

Elite-Physiques also takes pride in their results. Ms. Daniels believes that their clients are their best advertisement. When an Elite-Physiques client gets their body in great shape and people ask them how they got that great body they tell them at Elite-Physiques and that is the best advertisement that you can have. Being able to use different means of advertisement in this modern day and time is critical for any business. Elite-Physiques has positioned itself to become a force in the fitness industry by doing and using all means of advertisement necessary. As anyone knows a business cannot survive on advertisement alone. You also have to have someone who uses their knowledge and experience to push you forward. This young Entrepreneur is doing just that with Elite-Physiques. Ms. Daniels has taken Elite-Physiques and grown it in just a few years. She talked to me about when she first opened the business and how it was only this small space that she subleased on the outskirts of Randallstown, and now has expanded the center. She laughs as she tells me about her clients, who were with her and have seen the growth. She says, "they did not mind that we were in this small space, they did not complain at all". She also says "they told her don't get us wrong, we love the space that you have now, but we did not mind the smaller space either".

As we walked around the facility and she tells me and shows me the area that she first started in it reminds me of the town house that I grew up in. I go through my old neighborhood every now and again and as I ride by the old house I think to myself, how did we live in that small house. As we get older we grow and outgrow the areas that we once were apart of, but with growth comes the need for more space. We make due during the time that we are in that particular phase in our childhood or business, but as we and our businesses get older we expand. Well, Ms. Daniels and Elite-Physiques is expanding just fine. With expansion comes a need for more space. In business the need for more space means more square footage. It does not matter what industry you are in when you grow you need to acquire more space. In the case of Elite-Physiques they were no different. When you are a young entrepreneur and you have to do business with older businessmen and women they find it hard to believe that you are the person who owns a business. They keep looking for someone else and when they finally realize that there is no one else they can sometimes try and make it very difficult for you to do business with them.

The fitness industry is no different than any other industry when it comes to young entrepreneurs getting their due in business. Ms. Daniels learned this the hard way. Experiences such as this shows us that in this modern day and time many people are not ready to see young and gifted entrepreneurs such as Ms. Daniels be successful. Well, they have no choice in the matter because Ms. Daniels and others like her have made it clear that they are here to stay.

THE FUTURE

In order for us to move forward we must first know where we began. We must understand whose shoulders that we stand on. This reflection is not hard for Ms. Daniels and Elite-Physiques to do. Beginning with her vision, her mentor and investor, Mr. Banks, and her uncle, Mr. Eugene Daniels, Ms. Daniels used their initial investments to begin her visions work. "What these two men did for me was to invest in my dream, she says. It had to be more than a dream because as any entrepreneur will tell you that when you have investors they want to see a "plan", a business plan. Her investors wanted to see what her business looked like on paper. She emphasized to me that what they gave her was not a gift; it was a "loan". Investors want to know how they will get their money back. Well, I know that her two initial investors are well pleased in what has turned out to be a very good investment.

From the looks of things their investment seems to be growing and growing. Elite-Physiques is grabbing a strong hold in the Randallstown, Maryland community. It will not be long before this company begins to branch out and become the bigger vision that its creator wants it to be. Ms. Daniels hopes to one day grow Elite-Physiques into a multi-purpose facility. She hopes to be able to make fitness both a physical option as well as a mental option. Having people mentally healthy as well as physically healthy is what she wants to offer to individuals. Ms. Daniels believes being mentally fit is just as important as being physically fit. The more mentally fit that we are the more physically fit we can be. One's mentality has to change before their physical body can change. As the fitness industry goes through its paradigm shift, this young entrepreneur is securely navigating her industry and remaining true to the fitness industry roots. Her "Old Soul", "Old School", approach to fitness will help her and Elite-Physiques go a long way in the future. Wanting to make sure that her customers are satisfied with their results and genuinely enjoying seeing how happy her clients are when they look in the mirror or other people tell them that they look great, shows not only the love she has for what she does but also for the people that she impacts in fitness. Starting Elite-Physiques is not enough for Ms. Daniels.

She is not a talker but she is a doer. She is one of the now generation that does not just talk about doing something but goes out and does it. From starting Elite-Physiques to putting her company in the position to become one of the top fitness centers in the country. She is not just about making herself better but she is about making others better. Her heart is big and her vision is progressive. Moving forward and investing not only in herself but in the future of others. She does her part in bringing her employees along just as someone did with her but her plans are so much bigger. She tells me that her giving back has not begun yet.

Being supportive just as others were supportive of her is very important, but do not think that anything will be handed to you on a silver platter. You will have to earn it. From this author's perspective, Ms. Daniels has done more than earned it, she has built it and they are coming to Elite-Physiques to get it!

CHAPTER 4
FINANCIAL WELLNESS

HARRINE FREEMAN

CEO
H.E. FREEMAN ENTERPRISES

INTRODUCTION

Harrine Freeman is a member of the American Association of Daily Managers, the National Association of Woman Writers, SPAWN, IEEE, Woman In Technology, and the Women Network. She has provided credit repair counseling for issues such as bankruptcies, judgments, student loans, delinquent debts, repossessions, and much more. She has been a guest speaker at local churches, schools, national radio shows and fortune 100 companies.

Her experience began by repairing her own credit. She was $19,000 in debt and was making only $21,000 a year. She has been debt free for the past 10 years. In 2000, she began providing credit repair services to family and friends. In 2002, she began a credit repair and personal finance business and has helped thousands of clients of all ages and economic backgrounds go on to purchase homes, cars, start businesses and purchase investment property. She has a B.S. degree in Computer Science and is currently pursuing a Master's degree in Information Technology. She has been an IT professional for the past 13 years providing quality assurance, testing, and software development services to government and commercial businesses.

She has a giving spirit and continually gives back to her community by doing volunteer work. She writes frequently and has written technical documentation for the IEEE Instrumentation and Management Magazine, as well as written several ezine articles on personal finance. Her first book "How to Get out of Debt: Get an "A" Credit Rating for Free Using the System I've Used Successfully with Thousands of Clients was published by Adept Publishers and was available in bookstores in December 15, 2006. She currently lives in Washington DC.

As I mentioned in the previous chapter, America is overweight, I also believe that America is in debt. From the government to individual Americans, America is about to have a debt attack! This government has put us in a financial bind that will have an affect on us for years to come. The rich in this country are getting richer and the poor are getting poorer. Far too many people are living beyond their means. They spend the little money that they do have on houses that are over priced and cars that they can't afford, all in the name of keeping up with the "Jones". Well, America here is a news flash, the Jones' are broke too! When will we learn that we must get our financial houses in order. We have not gotten the message that our futures are in jeopardy and we must begin now to secure it.

If I have said it once I will say it again. We have to begin to understand how money works. Most people do not understand how there money works. They spend hours on a job, collecting paycheck after paycheck and continue to be broke. It is very much like the rat running on the exercise wheel in its cage, going nowhere. We will continue to be in the same financial difficulty if we do not educate ourselves on money. I know some of you are saying what does understanding money have to do with being in debt. Well if we understood our money better then most of us would not be in the financial crisis that we are in. There are some that may be in debt due to unforeseen circumstances, but there are quite a few of us who are in debt due to our own doing. I am a firm believer that the more educated people are the better decisions they will make.

Well, it is time for us to start making better decisions. It starts now!!! We will begin by eradicating the notion that all of us are poor. Not all of us are poor but there are a lot of us that are net worth challenged! Those who are net worth challenged must first know the difference between income and disposable income. When we know how much money is coming in and where our money is going we can better understand what it will take to get us off of debt life support. Well, in my search to find a person who has learned how money works, I was introduced to a woman that takes educating others on how money works and getting them off of debt life support seriously.

She is not only a person who delights in helping others become debt free but believes in teaching them how to stay that way. Her passion for getting people's financial wellness under control is unparallel. There are many credit counseling centers that you can go to but there is only one company that is not a credit counseling center but a Financial Wellness organization, and that company is **H.E. Freeman Enterprises**, owned and operated by Ms. Harrine Freeman.

BEGINNINGS

This Washington DC native began her formal years attending one of the model academic high schools, Benjamin Banneker High School in Washington DC. Ms. Freeman was a stellar student and took pride in the education that she gained. Once her high school education came to an end she would make her way to Hampton University in Hampton, Virginia, where she majored in Computer Science. She would attend Hampton for 2 years and then would return to Washington DC to finish at University of District of Columbia (UDC). With her degree in hand she would enter into the IT field and would stay continue on in her field of study. She has held several positions in the IT profession that includes: Software Tester, Business Analyst, Team Lead, Manager, Configuration Manager, and Developer. As you can see Ms. Freeman has built quite a resume in the computer science field. The computer science field would only be able to hold this budding entrepreneur back so long. Before the journey of entrepreneurship would call, Ms. Freeman would hear the ring tones of her creditors calling first.

Ms. Freeman says that about 10 years ago, when she was attending college she was beckoned to the tables that would be placed ever so strategically on the campus of her school. What was on these tables many of us who have been to college knows all to well. The tables were filled with brochures of these little plastic things that the representatives told us would be great for us. They told us that we could use it just like cash and all we had to do was pay it back on a monthly basis. They even told us that we did not have to pay some of them back all at once.

We could pay it back in minimum amounts. These little plastic things have gotten many of us former college students as well as grown adults into a lot of unfortunate debt. These credit card companies seek out young unsuspecting students and tell them all of the glorious things that they can buy with this plastic credit card and seek to get them in over their heads long before they even think about graduating.

It is upsetting to me that these credit card companies are allowed to speak to students about credit cards before they graduate from college. Most college students do not have a job, and if they do it is usually a part-time one at best. They do not have any extra money, unless mom or dad are sending them money. If you were like me your parents did not have any extra money to send to you while you were in school. You were scraping together dimes and quarters just to get a sandwich, or those nasty oodles of noodles, that I still hate to this day because I ate them so much back then. You had no means of income so how did these credit card companies expect you to pay back the debt that you would incur with this credit card.

Well Ms. Freeman was no different then any of the rest of us who ventured over to the table and signed up for a credit card. She says, "It went all down hill from there". Ms. Freeman said that many of her fellow students did not have jobs and the credit card companies knew that they would not be able to pay back the money that they would run up on those credit cards. She also stated that you must be 18 years or older in order to get approved for a credit card and many of them that got approved were not of age. They now have student credit cards that high school and college students can use. Students under age 18 must have their parents permission. Luckily for the students if they default on the credit card legally the credit card company cannot collect from the student because the company has to have a signed contract with an adult which is considered to be 18. However, if a parent co-signs a credit card for their child and the child does not pay on the account the parent will be held responsible to pay for the debt owed.

Once Ms. Freeman received her first credit card she would receive many more pre-approved credit cards in the mail and she did not hesitate to sign up for those as well. She would soon find herself having 13 credit cards and $11,000 in debt. Once she discovered that she was in this mountain of debt her mother would discover it as well. Ms. Freeman says that her mother sat her down to find out what was going on and tried to assist her daughter in getting out of this situation that she was in.

Her mother would call the credit card companies on her daughter's behalf and tried to explain the situation with her daughter not having a job and not being able to pay back the amounts due on the credit cards. When Ms. Freeman's mother tried to negotiate with the credit card companies Ms. Freeman says that the credit card companies told her mother that she could pay the bills for her. Well, of course Ms. Freeman's mother told them that she would not be paying them back because it was not her debt but they did not want to hear that. She would eventually have to sit herself down after realizing that she was getting herself into more and more debt and would have to buckle down to get from under all this debt. Ms. Freeman says that she finally started to call the credit card companies and would set up payment plans with them in order to begin to get herself out of the debt that she had piled up.

While in the midst of working on her debt she would encounter some bumps in the road. She would lose her job, of no fault of her own, and would find herself in even further debt. When it was all said and done she would be some $19,000 in debt. Ms. Freeman, being the strong woman that she is, would bounce back and would find another job and would even take on a part-time job to help her keep up with the payment plans that she had set with the credit card companies. As she puts it being in debt made her feel as if she was in bondage. There are many of us today who are still in the bondage of debt.

Ms. Freeman says that it was not easy but she has been debt free for the past 10 years. Once she was able to get out of debt Ms. Freeman would tell her friends and family about how she was able to become debt free. She says that one of her friends suggested to her that she should start her own business showing others how to become debt free as she did. Ms. Freeman says that she helped some of her co-workers and so she would take the advice of her friend and would heed the call to become an entrepreneur and help others in the process. She would start her business 5 years ago and has not looked back ever since. She then took some financial courses to learn more about her industry.

As a third generation entrepreneur Ms. Freeman didn't seek advice from her family but gained her advice and knowledge on her own which she feels proved more valuable to her because she was able to learn from her mistakes. She would not only start her own business she would also put pen to paper and would write a book that would show others how to get out of debt as she did. She would author the book "How To Get Out Of Debt: Get an "A" Credit rating for Free Using the System I've Used Successfully With Thousands Of Clients". It does not stop there though, she would not only author the book, she would self publish the book through her publishing company Adept Publishers. As you can see what the devil meant for evil God turned into good. Ms. Freeman's strong desire to not see others go through what she had to go through is the stirring force behind H.E. Freeman Enterprises and what she tries to impress upon people when she goes to speak with churches, fortune 100 companies, and other organizations.

THE INDUSTRY

The financial consulting business is on the rise. With more and more people going into net worth comas, there is a growing need for individuals that can enlighten people on getting themselves back to being in the credit black as opposed to being in the credit red. You see it on television and you can't go through any town without there being those who will tell you that they can show you or tell you how to get out of debt. The difference between them and Ms. Freeman and H.E. Freeman Enterprises is they will get you out of debt. Ms. Freeman teaches how to get out of debt and how to stay out of debt. Ms. Freeman believes that your customer service is a key aspect to being an entrepreneur. She believes that you can offer people your services without giving good customer service and that can have a very negative effect on your business. She tells me "that as a customer she will not do business with a company that does not give good customer service".

Her company offers something that most others do not. HE Freeman Enterprises. has established itself from others by teaching their clients how to talk to their creditors, balance their check books, and how to develop a budget. Ms. Freeman believes that people are in debt and do not know the appropriate resources to go to in order to get out of debt, nor do they know the laws and other rights that are in place for people trying to repair their credit and become debt free. In this day and time it is vitally important that people understand their money, and not do business with companies who just want to take your money.

When you can offer people something that will make them better off then when they came into your office you can go a long way. The credit restoration industry is filled with those who are chasing the dollar but there are a few companies in this industry who actually care about the financial wellness of individuals. H.E. Freeman Enterprises is a company that believes in serving their clients by always being educated about the industry, services, and being respectful, and focused on results.

As an entrepreneur Ms. Freeman believes that you must always be professional and you must treat people with courtesy. Many entrepreneurs today have gotten away from one of the basics of business and that is promptness. When you are scheduled to meet with someone you should be on time and ready for that person when they show up. You don't punch a clock when you work for yourself and the only people that you answer to are your clients. Your clients expect you to arrive when you say that you are going to be there.

They also expect you to do what you say you are going to do. What Ms. Freeman and the H.E. Freeman Enterprises offers to her clients is relative experience in what she is consulting them on. Some of the companies in the credit restoration industry have people working for them that have not had the experiences that the people that they are meeting with have, so as a consequence they cannot relate.

Well Ms. Freeman can relate to her clients because she has been where they are and knows exactly what it takes to get out. That is something that you will not get when you go to some of the other companies. Ms. Freeman says the credit industry has become more consumer friendly in the past several decades. The government passed laws that were specifically geared to help and protect consumers. They past the **Fair Debt Collections Practices Act and the Fair Credit Reporting Act.** Unfortunately, not many people are aware of these laws or do not know how these laws protect them. A company is not allowed to call someone before 8am nor can a company call someone after 9pm.

Companies cannot threaten you, be rude to you, nor can they pretend to be an attorney. In this day and time you have some companies that are so money hungry that they will use unethical means in order to get money so you have to be very careful and know your rights.

The credit industry is now moving towards making it more difficult for consumers to file for bankruptcy. The government passed a law in October 2005 making it harder for people to file for bankruptcy. There is even more strict criteria that you must meet in order for you to file for bankruptcy. Ms. Freeman also says that there is a new credit score that is being used that not a lot of people do not know about it. Most of us are familiar with FICO score, which is the credit score generally used in the industry to determine your credit worthiness. This new credit score in addition to the FICO score is called the vantage score. This new credit score was created by the three credit bureaus Equifax, Experian, and TransUnion. Ms. Freeman says that the way it works is that a lender or financial institution would request a credit score, then the three credit bureaus would have to go to FICO to request a credit score and then they in turn would give the scores to the lender. The three credit bureaus have created their own credit score so that they do not have to go through FICO. The disadvantage with this new credit score is that the grading system that they use is not the same as FICO. With the FICO score an 850 would be considered excellent, but with the Vantage system it is only considered very good, says Ms. Freeman. The scale gets lower as you go down it with the Vantage score. The scale for the Vantage credit score goes like this:

901-990 A score
801-900 B score
701-800 C score
601-699 D score
501-599 F score

The FICO credit score ranges as follows:
750-850 Excellent
740-680 Good
620-679 Fair
610 or below Fair

So, as you can see there is quite the disparity in the two credit scores. Also when you are looking at your credit score it is calculated based on 5 factors.

35% of your credit score is your payment history
30% of your credit score is the amount owed
15% of your credit score is length of credit
10% of your credit score is new credit
10% of your credit score is type of credit in use

It is crucial that we begin to understand what our credit means to us. You can't do much of anything these days without good credit. You will not be able to purchase a house, buy a car, or in some cases get a job. More and more employers are using credit to determine whether or not a persons hired. In this industry people can be standoffish in the beginning because they think that it is a scam. With all of the scandals and fabricated businesses out there today, it can be hard to show people that you are real and have their best interest at heart.

Ms. Freeman began her company by helping her friends, family and co-workers, which aided her in establishing a community presence. She took her own experience and desire to help others to start her business. Being a young entrepreneur you will find yourself more than likely needing start up capital. Where you get that capital will be up to you. You can use traditional means such as banks or grants, if they are available. You may also have to resort to non-traditional means such as going to friends and family, or other personal investors. Some of you may have to keep a regular job while growing your business. There is nothing wrong with doing that and there are many of us who have done that.

The credit restoration industry is on the incline. With so many people going into debt there are numerous potential clients. In the past few years it has been startling the number of people who are going into debt. The bankruptcy laws that were once kind to individuals have been revised. With companies such as H.E. Freeman Enterprises in the industry individuals will truly understand their options of getting out of debt, and hopefully staying out of debt. What Ms. Freeman loves about her industry is the satisfaction that she gets when her clients become debt free. Ms. Freeman says that when she helped her first client to become debt free she felt like she had just climbed Mount Everest. In this industry you must understand people and by understanding them you can get them to where they want to be much faster.

Ms. Freeman and the H.E. Freeman Enterprises family are constantly educating themselves on what people do with their money and why they do it. People's spending habits have become undisciplined. I heard on this talk radio program the other day that the average salary for an Asian-American was around $60k; White-Americans were just behind them somewhere in the upper 50's.

Then they said that the average Black-American's salary is $30k. I thought to myself, how is it that we as Black-American's make the least amount of money out of all of the ethnic groups, yet we are the largest consumers? One of the answers is discipline. The second is living beyond your means. These two characteristics are not only what plagues our communities but is what ails our country as a whole today. Most of the companies in this industry will not take the time to help their clients understand what it will take to become debt free and how living below your means is the beginning of staying debt free.

One company that I believe will do that is H.E. Freeman Enterprises. Educating people on money means that they may not be able to do things that they want to do. They will not be able to go places that they want to go to, but when they learn how it will benefit them in the long run then they will be much happier. It is extremely important that we understand where we are spending our money. If we understand where we are spending our money then we can better understand our financial situations and how to fix them.

Our salaries play a very important part in the debt that we are in. If the average salary in our community is only 30k then we must be very disciplined with our money. We still have not learned that lesson, but hopefully with Ms. Freeman and H.E. Freeman Enterprises we will begin to understand it.

As H.E. Freeman Enterprises enters into its adolescent years of business it has proven to the industry that doing things beyond the norm can work. Ms. Freeman has gained much respect from her clients as well as her community. Being a young entrepreneur has helped her because people can relate to her. She also believes that people feel comfortable with her due to the fact that she has experienced what they are going through. She also tells me that people are proud of what she is doing, which makes her feel good about what she does. I am a firm believer that we as entrepreneurs should enlighten, empower, and invest in the communities that we are a part of and Ms. Freeman is certainly doing that with class and style.

Since H.E. Freeman Enterprises is young Ms. Freeman believes that it can only get stronger. Preparing people to be equipped is what H.E. Freeman Enterprises does. H.E. Freeman Enterprises is about financial freedom, never being worried about bills, and creating financial wellness. The financial consulting industry is headed in the right direction with owners like Ms. Freeman. Using her practical experience as well as her relative experience has helped her to come to understand her business and her industry. When you are a young entrepreneur you can afford to take risk and chances that you might not take as an older one.

Ultimately as an entrepreneur, you are the one that has to make the final decision. You will make some good decisions and you will make some bad decisions. Keeping your bad decisions to a minimum is what we all strive for as businessmen and women. In the financial consulting business, making the right decisions is what your clients depend on. They look to you for direction and education. Ms. Freeman and H.E. Freeman Enterprises looks to educate their clients and to get them headed in the right direction. So far, that formula has worked for them and I believe will continue to work for them going into the future.

THE FUTURE

I am convinced that in this modern 21st century we as black men and woman must begin to leverage ourselves on three fronts. Those three fronts are the "Educational Divide", the "Digital Divide", and the "Financial Divide". When we can begin to understand that these three fronts are where we can begin to elevate ourselves and make a stronger mark in the global society. My mother once told me that her generation's fight was for civil rights and other lawful rights that we should have. They fought that battle so that we would not have to. She also told me that my generation has a different fight to fight and in a different way. Our fight as I stated earlier is educationally, technologically, and financially. We must fight to get our public educational systems in order. They have been neglected and it has been the cause of our communities decay.

In this modern technological era, it is crucial that we keep our communities up with the times. If we do not then we will begin to get left behind. The gap is widening and if we are not careful, we will find ourselves too far behind to catch up. Technology is advancing daily. We must not only educate ourselves but we must ensure that our children are technically savvy. You cannot be in business and not recognize the impact that technology has on your business. You must also realize the impact that the internet and other technical advances have on your business. These two divides that I have mentioned are two vital pieces to our overall leverage pie but they are connected by the third piece of that leverage pie the "Financial Divide".

The financial divide is a fight that has existed for many years. We now however, have a means to close that divide. One of those means is financial wellness, and understanding money. When you understand money, it opens you, your business, and your community to new levels. When we put our money to use effectively and collectively we can begin to influence change. We can affect change in our educational system, our political make up, and our communities. One company that I believe is trying to close that financial divide is Ms. Freeman and H.E. Freeman Enterprises. When you can influence a community in the way that HE Freeman Enterprises is you begin to change the face of that community.

I think that with the focus and the drive that Ms. Freeman has she will have a great impact on many of our communities in the near and distant future. Admiring individuals such as Earl Graves Sr., Bill Gates, Oprah Winfrey, Donald Trump and even Angelina Jolie. She says seeing their entrepreneurial spirit and there giving spirits has had a great influence on Ms. Freeman. Her desire to be able to better people is her goal for now and the future. It is not just good enough to own a home but we must also understand what that home can do for you. It is also not just about owning a business but what you do with that business.

For H.E. Freeman Enterprises the future looks bright. Eventually becoming a household name is inevitable. Being well grounded and having people's best interest at heart will take this company a long way. With their excited, motivated, focused, and poised leader, H.E. Freeman Enterprises is headed into the future with their bright lights on and will not stop until it has reached and taught everyone in its world the value of their money. When you think of your bills piling up, and there seems to be no end, just know that you can be debt free and the company that will rejoice with you when you accomplish it is H.E. Freeman Enterprises!

CHAPTER 5
INSPECTOR HOWARD

BRIAN "THE HAMMER" HOWARD

OWNER
HOWARD RESIDNETIAL SERVICES

INTRODUCTION

In 1987 I entered my freshmen year at the University Of Maryland Eastern Shore (UMES). The college experience at UMES is like no other. There is nothing like attending a Historically Black College. While there I gained lessons that I believe I would not have learned had I attended any other college. I also would not have met the people that I met had I not gone there. Most of my classmates have gone on and I am sure have paved very successful lives for themselves. When you are a Hawk you can't help but soar.

In 1989 I met a gentleman that I would become cool with and call my friend. I am pleased to be able to have entrepreneurs who are apart of this project that are college friends, fellow church members, and my family. It gives me great pleasure to be able to feature people who are not only making a difference in this society but are individuals that I know personally.

Over the past several years, the housing market has experienced a great surplus for sellers. It had become what those in the industry call a "Sellers Market". What this means is that there are not enough houses on the market to meet the demands. The prices of houses have gone beyond what I believe they should be valued. Houses that people bought for $100k are now valued at $200k. Houses that have no front or backyard and not even an acre of land on them are selling for well over $300k. It is absurd what houses are being priced for these days. Well that day is soon coming to an end.

The housing market is now beginning to experience a downward shift in its value. It is quickly becoming a buyers market again. Everyday I look at the paper and I see and read an article about the climate change in the housing industry. Sellers are becoming so desperate to sell their properties that they are willing to pay for the buyers closing cost. While this shift maybe good for buyers in certain respects they must also be careful to do their homework about the property that they are purchasing.

Buying a house is one of the biggest purchases that you will make in your lifetime, so it is imperative that you have that property scrutinized, examined and appraised from top to bottom. In order to have a property properly appraised I believe that you must have someone doing the appraisal that you feel comfortable with and you can trust. There is nothing more unnerving than to buy a house, have it appraised and then when you get in, you find out that there are more things wrong with it.

This can be a homeowner's worst nightmare. If you do not have someone who appraises your potential property, correctly, it can cost you more money than you ever anticipated. If an appraisal is done correctly, you can catch potential issues before you ever step inside the door and hold the seller accountable for the repairs. You also want to have an appraiser who you trust when you are purchasing a house so that you get the fair value of the house when you make an offer. Educating ourselves on the housing process is becoming more and more crucial.

There are houses being bought and sold everyday and how many of those houses do you believe had some one appraising them the correct way. Giving your customers honest value for their money is what most of us want today. No matter what industry or service that we seek, we want the best value for our dollar. This should be especially true when it comes to a home. No one wants to be blind-sided when it comes to having to put out money for seen or unforeseen issues in a house. The better prepared we are for those costs the more willing we may be to shell out the money for those repairs. It does not make it any easier for us to deal with the issues but at least we are aware of them.

Most people's incomes are over extended these days so what they spend their money on becomes even more important. Getting into a house can be very time consuming and frustrating. What can help to ease that frustration is knowing that the house that we purchased or are going to purchase is in the best shape possible. One person and company that prides itself in giving customers the comfort of knowing the true value of their potential purchase is someone I have known for over 15 years. I trusted him so much that when my mother went to purchase her condominium and needed to appraise the condominium and understand its true value, I called him. I knew that he would put the "Hammer" down when it came to doing the appraisal the right way. That person was Brian "The Hammer" Howard of **Howard Residential Services.**

BEGINNINGS

On the Westside of Baltimore is where this young entrepreneur grew up. Going to school at one of the West sides most notable public schools Walbrook Senior high. This warrior would gain his entrepreneurial spirit from his father who was an entrepreneur himself. His father taught him not to compromise himself and to be independent. One thing that Mr. Howard mentions is that even though his father gave him the insight of entrepreneurship he did not give him the knowledge of entrepreneurship, which I believe the generation before us has dropped the ball on. There are some individuals who have imparted to their children the insight and knowledge of entrepreneurship but as a whole it is something that is sorely needed with our generation.

Once he entered, college at the University of Maryland Eastern Shore Mr. Howard would begin to gain, as he called, his foundation for entrepreneurship. While he does not believe that college is a prerequisite for becoming an entrepreneur, he does believe that it gives you a knowledge base for establishing your business. His decree is "do not go to college to get a job, but go to college to get an education". When you use the education and knowledge that you gain from college it can help you in becoming a sound businessman or woman.

In college you are taught that once you come out you will get a good job and make a nice living, but once you get out into the "real world" you soon realize that what you were taught is nothing like what it really is. When you get into the "real world", you can spend a lifetime trying to get out of it. Those of us who figure out how to get out have the strong desire to have our own businesses. The desire to become an entrepreneur is not something that is given to you. It is something that I believe you either have or you don't. What has created that desire for Mr. Howard is knowing that the hard work that he put in for other companies could be well used for his company and his advancement. Realizing that the rat race of the corporate world can be a never-ending cycle and does not give you the sense of self- worth. Having your own business gives you that says Mr. Howard.

Using part-time jobs aided Mr. Howard in gaining his knowledge base for his own business. Many entrepreneurs have used their beginning jobs as a launching board for their thrust into entrepreneurship. There are not too many of us who can come right out of college or straight from high school and start our own business. We are too young and too green. I do not believe that any 19-25 year old person is mentally ready to handle a business or run a department. There is too much for you to learn.

Even myself, when I was the youngest supervisor for a major hotel chain, I was very much inexperienced. With Mr. Howard, it proved to be the same. Working for companies such as Home Depot gave him insights and experience that he would not have if he had not gone and worked for them. They have helped him to understand some of the things that he uses now for his Home Inspection business.

THE INDUSTRY

Most of the younger generation of entrepreneurs are first generation entrepreneurs. That means that we do not have people that groomed us for the businesses that we are running. Just as with any family up bringing having parents who groom their children for adulthood, their needs to be older entrepreneurs who prepare the young entrepreneurs on how to run their own business. I think that businesses as a whole would be a whole lot better off and better run if the older generation of business men/women would have taken the time to show this young generation how to run a successful business. This young generation is starving for leadership and because there is a lack of leadership, we have been forced to feel our way through the journey of entrepreneurship.

One of the downfalls to becoming a young business owner is that you do not understand business or money. It takes time for anyone to understand money. Most of us are not taught by our parents how money works or how a business should be run. Mr. Howard also talks about how the companies that he worked for kept him abreast of new material that was coming out which kept him up to date on materials that were either coming to the market or were on the market at that time.

These companies also provided him with accounting skills needed to run a business. As Mr. Howard came to realize that everything that you do with your business is based on accounting. From having to give a customer something for free to having something get damaged, Mr. Howard says, "it all shows up on the books". Taking that knowledge and being able to apply it to his business has helped him to better understand what running a business is really about. This goes back to the point that I made earlier about being young and inexperienced.

If Mr. Howard had not worked for Home Depot before starting his own business he would not have gained the knowledge that he gained or the experience that he got while working for them. While there may be exceptions to this rule of being too young and running your own business, for the most part you should gain some experience and knowledge and then venture into entrepreneurship. That is just what Mr. Howard has done with Howard Residential Services. He formed a solid foundation and is now building a company that has a structure that is built to succeed into the future.

The home inspection industry just as any other industry needs people with integrity. Home Inspection is an industry where people really count on the individual or company being honest with them. There are many inspectors out there who will perform their duties but to find one that will not only do an inspection but take the time to explain things to you is rare. That is what you get with Mr. Howard and Howard Residential Services. Howard Residential Services distinguishes itself from the rest of the Home Inspection Industry by helping people to understand the inspection process and what it means. He takes the time to tell them why certain things may need to be replaced or how long something may. He takes the time to let them know the cost of something now or in the future.

Mr. Howard told me that he takes great pride in his clients calling him back after they have moved into their home and how they saved a lot of money because of the way that he conducted his inspection. They let him know that they appreciated the way that he helped them save money. He says that it makes him feel good that he can have a positive impact on people's lives in a major way. He also talks about the flip side and how people have not listened to him and not taken his advice and then calls him back and let him know that something went wrong just as he told them it would. That is what customer service is all about. Giving your clients and customers the information and letting them make an informed decision.

Another way in which Howard Residential has distinguished itself from its fellow Home Inspection counterparts is Mr. Howard's understanding of his industries business cycle. What I mean by its business cycle is its busy season and its slow season. Mr. Howard knows when he gets most of his clients and when he will have a drop off in the number of clients. This is key in his industry because he has to be able to prepare himself during the busy season for the slow season. Being ill prepared for the slow season could mean that he would not be able to properly service those clients that he does get. This in turn could cause him to loose those customers.

This is key because that lack of service to those clients could filter into clients that he could possibly have during his busy season. Many businessmen and women do not take the time to understand their industry cycles. They have to be able to budget their money so that they are able to do things throughout the whole year and not just during their busy season. Not being properly prepared for the slow season could also mean the collapse of your business. I do not think that Mr. Howard and Howard Residential have to worry about that. He has a great understanding of his industry and passes that on to the clients that he has developed personal relationships with.

When Howard Residential first began some 10 years ago Mr. Howard says that there were a lot of Mom & Pop operations and no government regulations. Since then the government has imposed lead paint testing, radon testing, termite inspecting, and an increase in molding inspecting. Something Mr. Howard says that is going on now that did not occur when he first began is expert witnessing.

Expert witnessing is when an appraiser is called upon to appear in court on behalf of their customers. Mr. Howard also told me that the government entities are cashing in on the home inspection industry by hiring inspectors. The state hires home inspectors, which was not done 10 years ago. With the government getting more involved with the home inspection industry Mr. Howard sees regulation happening for his industry in the future.

Since there is no regulation in the home inspection industry today there is such a disparity in pricing. You can have one inspector who will charge you a low fee for a certain house and another inspector that will charge you a really high fee for the same inspection of the same house. Some inspectors will come out and do an inspection in less than an hour and some will do an inspection that lasts 4 hours. Mr. Howard says that regulation will begin to curtail some of the disparity in the industry. With regulation inspectors will be forced to adhere to standards that will be set. This will greatly impact the type of service that clients are given. At a minimum inspectors will have to inspect the roof, air conditioning system, heating system, electrical system, plumbing, and the foundation. Regulation will also force inspectors to spend a minimum of 2 hours at a property.

What Mr. Howard does that sets him and his company a part from some of the others in his industry is the service that he gives to his clients. Where some inspectors give their clients an inspection form as soon as they are finished, Mr. Howard gives his clients a Narrative Report. This report is completed after he goes to the property and takes notes. The report is an itemization of what needs to be fixed, an explanation of those items, his recommendations, and a list of the defects. He also gives a statement in each section, which evaluates that particular area as either being good, fair, or poor. What Howard Residential Services and Mr. Howard gives to his clients is a document that helps them on a couple of levels. It helps them as a buyer with purchasing the property.

Mr. Howard says, "You as the buyer can go to the seller and as a condition of the sale you can make the seller accountable for getting the deficient items fixed". Mr. Howard also knows that the buyer is able to use his document when they go to purchase their home owners insurance. The insurance company will ask the buyer certain questions that are related to the property and the document they get from Howard Residential Services will help them to answer the questions.

Howard Residential Services also distinguishes itself from its counter parts by using a flat rate system for his pricing. Mr. Howard says, "Whether it takes him 2 hours or 7 hours price is the same. He also does a full service inspection, both inside and outside. He also includes forecasting as a part of his inspections.

This will let the homeowner know what problems they can expect in 3-5 years with their property. The other thing that puts Mr. Howard above the rest of his industry is his educational background. With a degree in Construction Management he is able to have a level of understanding that most of his counterparts do not posses. This enables him to speak on the different trades that are involved in the construction industry, where his counterparts cannot speak on those matters to their clients.

The home inspection industry is full of individuals that will do the bare minimum for you, and then there are entrepreneurs like Mr. Howard who believe in taking customer service to the next level. With a thorough understanding of his industry and wanting to give his clients more insight into their homes, I am sure that this spirited entrepreneur will take Howard Residential Services even further. Making a difference in peoples lives in the manner that he does with each client stands out in an industry that takes care of people's most expensive investment. Even though the housing market is going through its ups and downs its nice to know that you have a company and an inspector that is willing to put service first and also teach you something about the investment that you made.

THE FUTURE

The housing industry's bubble is bursting. Houses are staying on the market that would not have been there five years ago. You have houses that are being sold for less since home owners are trying to get out of houses that they cannot afford, and as buyers you must have a thorough understanding of what you are getting into. Howard Residential Services will help you to be more informed on your investment so that you can make better decisions about the eventual return that you will get on that investment. Moving into the future can't be done without first understanding where you came from. For an entrepreneur like Mr. Howard in the industry he says that he did not need much capital to get started.

Being in the service industry he was able to work out of his home which as any entrepreneur knows will save you plenty of money. Being able to have access to capital is not one of our strong suits both Mr. Howard and I agree on. We have to be creative in the way that we gain access to capital. Sacrifice is the big word that Mr. Howard uses when he talks about being creative in gaining finances. "You may have to give up a few nights of going out ", says Mr. Howard in order to get to where you want to grow your business. You can also use the equity that you have in your house as he and some other entrepreneurs have done. Capital is out there we just have to figure out ways to get it. "You may even have to work another job to get yourself to where you want your business to be in the beginning", Mr. Howard says.

In order to move into the future you also have to have direction. In the beginning Mr. Howard admits that he did not have a plan. He got into the industry and found out that there was more to the industry then he expected. By doing his research and becoming certified in his industry prepared him for the 10 years of service that he has been providing and will no doubt continue to aid him in the future. With home ownership on the rise there are a plethora of clients out there for Mr. Howard and Howard Residential Services to gain. Since the industry is so crowded people have a number of inspectors to pick from. If regulation comes into this industry Mr. Howard believes that this will filter out a lot of his competition. Howard Residential Services in the future plans to be a one-stop shop.

In this day and time I believe that it is essential to a company's survival to expand to be able to offer its clients additional services and Howard Residential is doing that by offering its clients, appraisals, termite service, lead, water, and mold testing and random inspections. Growing from offering his clients basic home inspections to being able to offer them a diverse amount of services will help to create a stronger future for Howard Residential Services.

Mr. Howard also wants to include environmental services to his portfolio of services for his company. With advances in technology being made quickly in this industry Mr. Howard believes that this will allow him to offer other services that he would not be able to offer without the equipment and technology that has come along. Having the most modern equipment will enable Mr. Howard to offer his clients even more education and knowledge about their home before they purchase it.

Listening to where Howard Residential is headed makes the future for the Home Inspection Industry safe in its care. When you have an owner and company that not only cares about themselves but cares even more about their clients it makes me feel safe to say that with the "Hammer" doing your inspections you are definitely in good hands, and that's not AllState either! If making a lasting impression is what Mr. Howard is looking to do, his legacy is certainly safe with how he does business.

I am impressed with the service that Mr. Howard gives to his customers. In a time where customer service is being forgot by many business owners, Mr. Howard and Howard Residential has shown that the customer truly matters. So as you ride around the city of Baltimore and possibly the surrounding areas and you are looking at a building or a house, just know that, the "Hammer" just may have inspected it.

CHAPTER 6
BEAUTY FROM INSIDE OUT

LISA ENNIS

CREATIVE DIRECTOR
ECCENTRIC'S
THE SPA SANCTUARY

INTRODUCTION

Close your eyes and imagine that you have escaped from the stress and hassle of your daily routine. Instead, you are lying on a beautiful white sandy beach somewhere in the middle of the Caribbean Sea. You let your body completely relax while soaking up the warm rays of the sun as you listen to the sounds of the gently rolling waves and the steel drum band in the distance, you wish you could achieve this feeling of total peace without traveling hundreds of miles away from home. Thanks to the wonderful vision of Lisa Ennis - you can! This wish has been granted for residents of Odenton, Maryland and the surrounding areas. Ms. Ennis, who was inspired by the soothing and relaxing environment of the Caribbean Islands, opened Eccentric's -The Spa Sanctuary in the fall of 2003. As clients enjoy the services in this Caribbean themed salon and day spa, they are immersed in the island atmosphere, surrounded by wall murals of beach landscapes, while the sounds of island rhythms fill the air.

Before opening Eccentric's -The Spa Sanctuary, Ms. Ennis owned a very successful full-service hairstyling salon for nine years that featured dynamic haircuts, hairstyles, hair color, permanent waves, relaxers, manicures, pedicures, makeup, applications and waxing services. Ms. Ennis closely followed the emerging new day spa trends in the professional beauty industry that went beyond hair and advocated the philosophy that beauty was much more than the outer physical self; it was a total body experience. The desire to promote inner peace and well being of the soul within her clients as well as to provide total beauty care and wellness services, prompted Ms. Ennis to launch the new Eccentric's –The Spa Sanctuary.

With the ultimate goal of providing "A soothing solution for a stressful world", says Ms. Ennis. Ms. Ennis has added exciting new skincare and spa therapy services to the hair care services that dominated the menu at her former salon. Clients may choose from a variety of personalized facials based on skin types and desired results, including the Eccentric's Signature Facial, Aromatherapy Facial, Acne Facial and Multivitamin Power Treatment. Additional skincare customization is available with add-on services such as hydroxyl acid exfoliation, revitalizing eye treatments, contour masques and paraffin wax treatments.

The new spa treatments are based on a combination of ancient and modern revitalizing therapies designed to detoxify the body, un-wind the mind and revitalize the skin, and include the Hydro-Active Mineral Salt Scrub. Enzymatic Sea Mud Wrap and Body Therapy Hydro-Pack. Eccentric's -The Spa Sanctuary also offers several treatments that focus on the specific skin care needs and concerns of men, such as the Caribbean Facial that helps alleviate shaving bumps and skin irritations. Hair removal, nail care and makeup application are also available. These special hair, skin, nail and spa services are offered in packages that rejuvenate the body from head to toe and allow clients to indulge in a day of beauty and relaxation.

As a minority salon owner, Ms. Ennis has composed a team of talented, multicultural hairstylists; aestheticians and nail technicians who work together to design a signature look for each client. The diversity of this team allows ESS to offer the latest trends in services for clients of every age, culture and ethnicity. To ensure that clients receive quality service with every visit, all of their salon and spa professionals participate in an ongoing advanced training program that encourages professional and personal development for both technical and customer service skills.

Every new employee, regardless of experience, goes through a one- month training program to acclimate them to the Eccentric's -The Spa Sanctuary culture. Top nationally respected industry educators are also frequently invited to the salon to share their knowledge with the staff. To encourage staff to meet and exceed salon as well as personal goals. Ms. Ennis has hired motivational coach Pastor James Rollins to lead weekly inspirational sessions at the salon.

Ms. Ennis has been a favorite hairstylist of local clients for years. The innovative salon, hair, skin, nail and spa services offered by Eccentric's –The Spa Sanctuary have become an instantaneous new success story. Ms. Ennis has been nationally recognized as a talented hairstylist by top fashion and beauty publications such as Celebrity 101 Hairstyles, Salon Ovations, Salon Today, and Black Hair Actress Magazines as well as Passions International Stylebooks. Eccentric's –The Spa Sanctuary has also been recognized as one of the "Top Hair color Salons in the USA" by Celebrity 101 Hairstyles Magazine.

In the mid 1800's there was a woman by the name of Sarah Breedlove. Ms. Breedlove grew up in the south and moved north once she got older. She was a strong woman and found herself surrounded by other women who would expose her to a completely new way of thinking. Through her trek to the north, Ms. Breedlove experienced some turbulent times that would change the course of her life. Ms. Breedlove began to have difficulty with her hair falling out. She tried different counteragents but to no avail, so she came up with her own hair care product to heal her scalp. After inventing this new hair care product, she started her own business and traveled around the country selling her products in churches, and lodges. She also developed business strategies that would grow her business even further.

With a successful business, she wanted to teach others how to care for hair so she opened a school that groomed others to treat hair. In addition to a school, she opened a factory that produced her hair care products. She also opened a hair and manicure salon. This great businesswoman went on to grow her business nationwide as well as globally. She established herself as one of the most admired woman of color in history.

Women of this generation talk about Oprah Winfrey, but without Ms. Sarah Breedlove, also known to us as Madame C.J. Walker, there would be no Oprah Winfrey, or any other woman business owner. Madame C.J. Walker set the standard for woman in business and specifically women in the hair care industry. Without her there is no them.

I was introduced to a woman who brought back the spirit of women in business as Madame C.J. Walker represented. She has taken what was introduced to us by Ms. Walker and moved it to the next level. What this woman has done is captured the essence of service and devotion. She not only wants to give women a beauty that makes them look good on the outside but she wants to give them a beauty that can be seen on the inside as well.

When I was privileged to meet this entrepreneur I was taken by her sincere desire to not only be an entrepreneur but to show others how to be entrepreneurs, and that is what Madame C.J. Walker accomplished in her generation and I have no doubt that this entrepreneur will do the same in her generation. Meet Ms. Lisa Ennis of **Eccentric's - The Spa Sanctuary.**

BEGINNINGS

In the small town of Crofton, Maryland is where our next entrepreneur got her start. Growing up in the same community where she now owns a business in is something special for Ms. Ennis. She went to Arundel High school in the Crofton area and is now back where it all started. Ms. Ennis says that Crofton is a very small area and the area where she grew up everyone knew each other and there was one church that everyone attended. Growing up her desire was to do hair. She had people who tried to discourage her from wanting to do this but she would not be denied. Ms. Ennis believes that everyone is born with a passion for something, and it is up to you to tap into that passion and bring it out.

"Having a salon in the same town that I grew up in is something that I could have never imagined", Ms. Ennis says. She says this because the Crofton/Odenton area was not the "cool" place to be. She sees the area up and coming now and the potential that it has for the future. Back in the day the Crofton/Odenton area had its share of racism, but now it is showing some good growth potential Ms. Ennis admits. Gaining her experience from a salon that she initially worked for, Ms. Ennis says that she was very comfortable where she was and had no intensions on opening her own salon at first. "It was too much responsibility", she says. As more and more of her clients started to inquire of her when she was going to open her own salon she began to give it some serious thought.

As she began to investigate more about owning her own salon she found that there were things that she needed to do. The first thing she needed was a "Business Plan". Developing a business plan is something that every entrepreneur should do. I heard it said, "Those who fail to plan, plan to fail". This statement holds true especially in the business world. How can you get to where you are going if you don't know how to get there? You may not use every aspect of your business plan but it will at least give you a physical map of where your business is going and how you plan to get there. It will also give you something to look back on to see how you have progressed your business and if there are some changes that need to be made.

With the assistance of a family friend Ms. Ennis put together her business plan and had the family friend look over the document so that it would be ready to be presented to the financial institutions where she would go to for her start up capital. The family friend was a budding attorney so it was a win/win situation for both of them. Let this be a lesson to the budding entrepreneurs out there. You can find creative ways to get your business off the ground. You must use all of the resources that you have at your disposal. This can help you as well as those individuals that you may assist. The first bank that Ms. Ennis went to turned her down but that would not stop her from pursuing her vision.

She eventually secured a small business loan to start her business. She was able to secure the loan due to her job stability and excellent credit. This is also something that young entrepreneurs must understand. <u>You must have good credit</u>. Your credit history is very important when you are planning to start a business. Your investors, whether they are traditional or non-traditional, will want to know that the business that they are investing in is in secure hands. The only things that you have to show for that security are your work history, and your credit history. They are not only important from a business perspective but are important from a personal perspective.

As you mature in your entrepreneurship career you will find out that your credit is one of your most valued assets. Whether you are going to have a new business or are looking to grow a business your credit will speak volumes for you. The value of my credit has become even more evident to me as I am getting older. When we are in our twenties we do not even think about our credit report or our FICO score. These are two things that young entrepreneurs need to grasp and understand now. There are three agencies that you get your credit report from; they are Experian, TransUnion, and Equifax. Each of these credit agencies provide credit reports that you need to get each year. You do not want to get just one because there maybe something on one that is not on another. You also want to get your FICO score. This score will tell you where you fall in regards to your credit rating.

As you can see you must keep your score at an acceptable rating in order to be able to qualify for any type of loans from financial institutions. They want to know that if they lend you any amount of money that you will be able to pay it back to them. Being able to secure a small business loan was a big step in Ms. Ennis getting her business off the ground. Another step that Ms. Ennis took to help with her business was attending Anne Arundel Community College and entering The UCLA Anderson School of Management. They have a program for Entrepreneurs who have their own beauty salons.

They send you information in the mail that you have to complete by a certain time period and then you attend their center for a week and take a class from 7:00am-9:30pm. You are divided into groups and have a different task that must be completed. They use your life experiences along with the credits that you completed in the program to complete the requirements you need to receive your business degree. Ms. Ennis has used the tools that she gained from that business program along with her artistic talent and built a gem of a business.

THE INDUSTRY

"It's not about us" is what Ms. Ennis believes her business and industry is all about. Understanding that you are here to serve is what we as business owners must realize, and we must begin to get back to the servant and leader mentality. Christ taught us that in order to lead someone you must first serve them. When you put your customer first in business, and you seek to serve them, you will find that your company will grow. Ms. Ennis believes, customers can tell when they are being put first by a business and when they are being treated as just another dollar added to a company's bottom line.

Ms. Ennis talks about when she first started her business there were not as many hair designers as there are now. When she first began it was a very serious business, and people took hair designing to heart. The people now in the industry do not seem to take it as serious as Ms. Ennis and her generation. She says that when she volunteers at the hair schools there are more students but only a small percentage of those students will continue in the industry.

The hair design industry is an industry that some people outside of the industry do not feel is an industry that should be taken seriously. It appalls me when I see individuals that look down on a particular industry or business as not being legitimate or not a serious career. If we did not have individuals that owned their own beauty salons such as Ms. Ennis then where would a woman be able to go to get their beauty needs met.

Any business or industry, that is legitimate, should be looked as a serious industry or business. It may not be the one that you choose but that does not make it any less of a business. Even within the industry there are those who Ms. Ennis believes do not take it seriously. "They see it as a way to get quick money and move on to the next thing". The people in the industry have to take it seriously before anyone outside of the industry will. There are many underground salons as Ms. Ennis describes them, which are not licensed salons therefore the procedures and practices are not on a professional level.

This will cause a problem for the industry because it may cause the industry to be deregulated. Since you have so many salons operating underground already it will be seen as not a big deal if it is deregulated. The thing that makes Ms. Ennis and the Eccentric's family different from others in her industry is that she takes each clients seriously. Even if her clients do not take what they do seriously they take them seriously.

As Ms. Ennis puts it, there is a difference between a "shop" and a "salon". At Eccentric's you are entering a professional environment and you will be treated that way from the time you make an appointment to the time you leave the salon. So many of our businesses today have forgotten about the customer but at Eccentric's the atmosphere and the service is all for the customer. Ms. Ennis says that what makes them different than others in the industry is the mindset that she has created at Eccentric's. They have developed "Soothing Solutions to a Stressful World". They not only treat the outer beauty they also treat the inner beauty.

What Ms. Ennis and the rest of the Eccentric's staff have created is a place where you can come and not only get your hair, and nails treated, but you can also get your body treated as well. From the customized skin care to the Caribbean Skin Care & Body Spa Treatments, to Reflexology, to the Bridal Services, you can get just what your body needs. Eccentric's -The Spa Sanctuary, also sets itself apart by the treatment of its internal customers. Ms. Ennis promotes financial freedom for her employees. Ms. Ennis wants to see her employees be successful as well. She has a program instituted for her company that allows for a financial mentor to come in and mentors her employees about how to spend their money and get out of debt. Nothing upsets Ms. Ennis more than to see her employees spending their money as fast as they are making it. What Ms. Ennis stresses with her employees is financial freedom and understanding what that means.

Some of the employees are not used to working in this type of environment with this type of structure in this type of industry, and that can be challenging for them at times, Ms. Ennis says. Some employees welcome the structure because it is something that they do not see at any other salon they have worked for. In all of the structure and programs that Ms. Ennis offers to her employees she wants them to be able to build wealth. By building wealth they will be able to take care of their families, and possibly open their own salon one day. Working together for the common goal is what Ms. Ennis has created at Eccentric's -The Spa Sanctuary.

Having the one-on-one financial coaching, is something that you will not find at any other company or in any other industry that I know of and that definitely separates Eccentric's - The Spa

Sanctuary from their competitors. In this day and time when people's finances are out of order it is important that the employees that work for you are emotionally and financially well. Eccentric's - The Spa Sanctuary, also has created a very relaxed atmosphere by having a Caribbean Theme. They serve Lemonade, and water as opposed to coffee and tea. They also play Caribbean music, which helps the customers feel comfortable from the time that they walk through the doors. To also help with employee motivation and team building, they have a theme day. Every other month an employee picks a theme and they dress up and bring in food that goes along with that particular theme.

"This team building idea goes over really well with the employees as well as the customers", Ms. Ennis says. She said that they did themes of different countries one time and they had to research the country and culture, so that they would know a little something about that part of the world. This also helped them to learn about other cultures and countries. Who would have thought that you could go to a salon and be taught about another country's culture?

Ms. Ennis also says that the clients love the themed events because they get to look forward to what the salon will be doing next. With innovative ideas like this it is no wonder Ms. Ennis is a very respectful, honest, genuine, and endearing person and is one of the special gems in her industry. The passion and compassion that she has for her clients and employees is something to be admired.

THE FUTURE

With Ms. Ennis and Eccentric's - The Spa Sanctuary it is more than just about the "dollar". Many businesses do not succeed because they are all about the dollar as opposed to the customers. Ms. Ennis believes that there are many entrepreneurs that can do the jobs that they do, but to be successful you have to be sure that you are bringing in more money then you are spending, and when you are focused on the "dollar", you usually do not do that. If your focus is only on the almighty dollar then you will not be able to take your business to the next level. In order to be able to get your business to the next level you must also surround yourself with like-minded people. For an entrepreneur being around other entrepreneurs who are as motivated as you are can keep you invigorated and also give you insights into innovative ideas for your business. There is nothing that will kill a person's creativity faster then being surrounded by negative people. This includes family, friends, church members or employees.

It is imperative that we understand how powerful an impact people that we surround ourselves with have. They can be a great help or a great hindrance to the direction that you and your business will go. One of the other things that deter us from starting our own business or even growing our business is access to capital. In order for us to use the traditional means of getting the capital that we need, Ms. Ennis talked about the importance of your credit. Credit is a huge indicator to lenders to determine if you should be approved for a loan and being able to show the lending institutions that you have the ability to pay back the money that you borrow from them. The better the credit rating the lower the risk you are to them. Even with non-traditional means of gaining access to capital you will need to show the venture capitalist or angel investors that you have a viable business and that it is worth them investing in. In this day and time we have to be creative in how we gain capital.

Ms. Ennis believes, being a young black woman entrepreneur does not make things easy for her in this industry or any other industry. It makes it easy in some respects because it acts as two minorities, but overall it is very challenging. Not being afraid to try different ideas and do different things is what will take Ms. Ennis and the Eccentric's -The Spa Sanctuary family into the future. Eccentric's has a fearless leader who is not afraid of doing what needs to be done. As Ms. Ennis puts it, "if I don't do it, then who else will"?

One of the main focuses that Ms. Ennis has for Eccentric's -The Spa Sanctuary, is making her industry more professional by visiting other salons and seeing how they run their businesses. Respecting your craft is what she is trying to instill in others who have their own shops or salons. Being on the board of one of the schools is one of the ways that she is able to change the way that the students think about this industry.

Being able to leave behind a legacy of wealth and being real is what is important to Ms. Ennis. She wants to be able to invest back into those who are coming behind her by giving them access to capital that she was not able to have access to through a foundation. It is important to Ms. Ennis that the legacy of professionalism is kept alive in her industry. If those in her industry do not take the time to nurture the entrepreneurs coming behind them then the hair care industry will be left in the hands of those who will not take the industry to the next level. It will be filled with individuals who put professionalism on the back burner and the dollar in the forefront of their minds. Moving Eccentric's -The Spa Sanctuary to the next level will also entail them growing into more than one location. Growing is a part of any successful business agenda. Being able to have Eccentric's -The Spa Sanctuary in multiple locations will do nothing but be a pleasant asset to the communities that it will eventually be apart of. With her passion for her industry and the love that she holds deep inside for professionalism,

Ms. Ennis also hopes to offer those in her industry a guide to running a successful salon. By being a diverse company and offering different services, Eccentric's -The Spa Sanctuary is grooming itself to be a mainstay for years to come. One of the things that Ms. Ennis believes that we must do in order to move into the future is also being a "doing generation". By building relationships with your team you are able to show them that we are all in this together.

If you can write it down and then follow up on what it is that you want to accomplish this will help this generation go from a talking generation to a doing generation. From the looks of it Ms. Ennis and Eccentric's -The Spa Sanctuary is definitely apart of the doing generation. In the spirit of Madame C.J. Walker, a woman who had a sincere desire to be successful, but also had a desire to help others become successful as well, Ms. Ennis has picked up the torch and is carrying it well into the future.

CHAPTER 7
J-CLASS

JERONDA T. DAVIS, MS, MDIV.

PRESIDENT
LIBERTY CONSULTING SERVICES

INTRODUCTION

Jeronda T. Davis is the founder and president of Liberty Consulting Services. She has over 10 years of technical writing experience for academic institutions, community and faith-based organizations, government contractors, and public and private sectors. Ms. Davis also offers over 10 years of experience conducting training, seminars, workshops, and health education on topics such as HIV/AIDS, substance abuse prevention, women and HIV, the Black church and HIV/AIDS, counseling techniques, ethical issues in clinical practice, cultural diversity, understanding African American culture, partner violence, marriage and family therapy, and others.

Previous clients include Morehouse School of Medicine, American Association for Marriage and Family Therapy/Commission on Accreditation for Marriage and Family Therapy Education, The MayaTech Corporation, Whitman Walker Clinic, House of Ruth, Greater Mount Calvary Holy Church/CATAADA House, University of Maryland, Howard University, and SAHSA Bruce.

Ms. Davis is a sought after consultant and speaker. She has appeared on numerous television and radio programs with local and national stations, such as News Channel 8, NBC4 with Joe Krebs, ABC World News Tonight, Black Entertainment Television, WPGC 95.5 FM, and WOL 1450 AM. Additionally, she has conducted two radio broadcasts that were aired on the continent of Africa.

Ms. Davis is a licensed minister through the Mount Calvary Holy Churches of America, where Bishop Alfred Owens, Jr. and Evangelist Susie Owens are the pastors. After seven years, she continues to provide family counseling and training at

CATAADA House, an outpatient drug and alcohol program of the Greater Mount Calvary Holy Church.

Ms. Davis is currently enrolled in a PhD program in social work at The Catholic University of America in Washington, DC. She received her BA degree in Psychology from Auburn University; an MS degree in Marriage and Family Therapy, also from Auburn University; and an MDiv in Theology from Howard University.

In her spare time, Ms. Davis enjoys creative writing. Since childhood, she has been a lover of the written and spoken word. Ms. Davis maintains a collection of over 100 poems and she often shares her poetry during open mike sessions at various poetry circuits throughout the Washington, DC metropolitan area.

In addition to being the founder and president for Liberty Consulting Services, LLC, Ms. Davis is also an adjunct professor at Prince Georges Community College and an HIV specialist at the Howard University Student Health Center.

Ms. Davis is the eldest of three siblings and the proud aunt of Christopher Isaac Avery and Tyah Davis. She currently resides in Upper Marlboro, MD.

If I were to say the words Mercedez-Benz to you, your first thought would probably be class, sophistication, style, prestige, longevity, and privilege. A few years ago I was attending a meeting for an organization that I was the Executive Director for at the time. After the meeting there was an opportunity to mingle and to talk with those who had attended the meeting. I happened to meet a young lady who not only captured me with her beauty but also captured me with her class and style. She had an aura about her that was not like anyone else that had attended the meeting. She struck me as a woman of distinction and determination.

As we conversed we found that we both had a love for the spoken word. We each have written our share of poetry, and performed at different venues. We struck up a friendship and a mutual respect for each other that individuals gain as they grow. I have met very few people who impress me, but when I met this young entrepreneur, I was impressed. Her intellect is second to none, her dedication is ever present, her style is like no one else, and her spirit is full with the Lord. As a young man my mother taught me the importance of the people that you allow into your space. Those individuals that you allow to be apart of your circle can be either a positive part of what happens to you or can bring so much negativity into your life that you don't know whether you are coming or going. I am glad that this entrepreneur has had a positive impact in my life. In life you need people that you can have great conversations with and individuals that are about moving in a forward direction.

In a day and time when people and organizations need help with their health and well being, it is vitally important that you have someone that possesses the technical skills to help those people and those organizations get back on the right track. People and organizations cannot afford to be misguided in what is the best direction for them. There are firms that will come in and do an evaluation for you, sit with you, and give you a bunch of data that will assist you.

Then there are firms that take special pride in what they do and will give you service that goes beyond your expectation. Knowing and understanding your organization or even yourself is sometimes not easy, and having someone looking from the outside in can give you a different perspective. Some organizations are beginning to realize that some employees may need to be educated on different aspects of life. Organizations need to be sure that their employees are healthy both physically and mentally. In this day and time we have individuals that have no regard for themselves nor do they have any regard for others. We are in need of a self-esteem makeover. Getting people to look at themselves is not an easy task. People are quick to point the finger at anyone but themselves. They do not want to take responsibility for their actions.

Whether it is an organization doing an internal evaluation or an individual doing a personal evaluation, there needs to be someone who can assist those organizations or individuals in that task. That person or firm must be trustworthy, competent, honest, and reliable. When I think over my career and some of the events that have occurred in the organizations that I was employed offered to us, I see the importance of that service now.

It takes a special person to be able to guide others out of certain issues. When it comes to dealing with this special type of consulting there is only one person and firm that comes to my mind. That person defines intelligence, elegance, integrity, and style. She is someone that personifies class. B-Smith may do it with style but this young entrepreneur does it with class. Meet the J-CLASS of **Liberty Consulting Services**, Ms. Jeronda T. Davis.

BEGINNINGS

This southern entrepreneur was born and raised in Alabama. The southern belle of Liberty Consulting Services, started out young and gifted while being the oldest sibling in the house. As some will attest, when you are the oldest child you set the standard for the rest of the siblings. We look up to our older brothers or sisters because they get to do everything before we get to and they get to set the standard that most of us will follow. Ms. Davis grew up in the south, which is evident in the southern soul that she personifies in her values, ethics, and demeanor.

Being the oldest child can be a daunting task because you are the one who is looked to out of all the other siblings. You are expected to help your parents when you are young and when they get older. You go from being the child to having to look after your little brother or sister. Your academic achievements or shortcomings are looked at more closely than anyone else's, when you are the first born, because those who come behind you may follow the path that you take.

While growing up in the south Ms. Davis earned her Bachelors degree in Psychology from Auburn University, her Masters degree in Marriage and Family Therapy, also from Auburn University, so as you can see education plays a very important role in this young entrepreneurs life. Serving the Lord has always been near and dear to this entrepreneur, which is why she holds a Masters of Divinity degree from Howard University. When you think of your entrepreneurship journey and the different aspects of what you have to offer your industry you have to be a very diverse individual. You must be talented in one respect and able to learn quickly on the other. The more that you have to offer to your company as an entrepreneur the more successful you will be. Ms. Davis learned this early on. Having the understanding that she would need to have the educational foundation to build her vision is something that not all young entrepreneurs understand.

Being a diverse individual helped to make Ms. Davis a stronger asset to her business when she decided to embark on that challenge almost two years ago. As young entrepreneurs we must have the intestinal fortitude to make decisions and do things now that will positively impact the future of our businesses. Ms. Davis not only saw the short-term goal of her business but also sees the long-term mission of where she wanted to take Liberty Consulting Services.

The more we look at the bigger picture to make our decisions the better off we will be as entrepreneurs and as individual businesses. Our businesses will go through stages and we have to know what they are and recognize the pieces that have to be put together so the company will be able to have a foundation, get stronger and move into the future. Ms. Davis has a plan for Liberty Consulting Services and she is sticking to it.

THE INDUSTRY

The world we live in is fast becoming out of control. When you look at the different businesses that are so corruptly run, along with the instability of the employees, it leaves one to wonder if there is any hope. So many industries are full of despair and unkindness. As businessmen and women there is a need for an evaluation of our systems and values. The young entrepreneurs of this day and time have to set a new standard of doing business. The days of working hard have to be brought back and a sincere desire to be over achievers must be taught and instilled into the work force. Being a structured organization has been long forgotten and has been replaced with inconsistency and callousness.

However, there is a woman and a firm that is geared to bring back the integrity, honesty, and order in the work force. Liberty Consulting Services is a company that will bring order to an organization and give you the ability to succeed as a business. Being able to assist businesses with reports, grants, or manuals is crucial in this day and time. In order to get grants from our government or any other organization you have to know how to put that proposal on paper. You have to know what the investors are looking for and you must be able to make sure that you are qualifying for the grants that you are applying for. Getting reports in order plays an important role for your company because you are able to get an understanding of where you are and where you are going, and more importantly how you are going to get there.

Liberty Consulting Services is geared to do that for its clients. What makes Liberty Consulting Services and its fearless leader unique is the diversity that they bring to the table. As we have learned previously Ms. Davis is a very diverse entrepreneur, and her company has that same diversity. Liberty Consulting Services is a business that consists of many different aspects. It is divided into a three-tier company.

They offer Technical Writing services, Training, and Counseling. Each branch of the business offers services that attract different types of clients. As any good entrepreneur knows the more you have to offer as a company the better off you will be. I will continue to emphasize this point throughout this whole book until everyone who reads this book gets this message about business. The first tier of Liberty Consulting Services is Technical Writing, which entails: Resumes, Grant Proposals, Reports, Manuals, and Editing.

With these services it serves both individual clients, faith-based and non-faith-based as well as corporate clients. The second tier of services that Ms. Davis and Liberty Consulting Services offers is Training, which includes: Health Education, Disease Prevention, Cultural Competency, Substance Abuse, Women's health, Partner Violence, Self-Esteem, Time-Management,Goal-Setting, Confidentiality/Privacy, Counseling, Group Therapy, Techniques, and Employment Readiness.

The third tier of services that this caring consulting firm offers is counseling, which includes: Counseling for individuals, Families, Couples, and Groups. As you can see Ms. Davis has designed Liberty Consulting Services to be a full service-consulting firm that touches both the private and public sectors. The last aspect, but certainly not least, that makes Liberty Consulting Services special and unique is that it is a faith-based company. Just like its leader the company has its foundation in God.

What Ms. Davis represents is the same thing that her company represents, and that is the Lord. An organization is only as strong as its leader, and the leader of this company serves notice that the Lord comes first with her and he will come first with the business as well. I know that there are some who may not believe in talking about God when it comes to business but for those of us who do believe in God, he is apart of everything that we do.

Learning your nitch is what will help you to be a successful entrepreneur, Ms. Davis says. If you are not good at writing then you don't want to try and write a book. Understanding who you are, what your business is and how it will fit into your particular industry will help you define where you fit in. Distinguishing yourself from your competitors is what will make your business a success or will cause it to fail. "It is fine to want to do well but do you have the training and background to be successful Ms. Davis says, Being able to help others and finding a unique way to do that is what Ms. Davis and Liberty Consulting Services is doing. It gives you more credibility and gets people's attention when you show them that you have been properly trained and educated in the industry you are in, Ms. Davis says.

Being a company that crosses into different industries can be an asset to a business and Liberty Consulting Services has placed itself in a positive position for both now and in the future. When you take on the business of helping others understand themselves or putting proposals together for them they are entrusting to you their faith in your abilities and talents. You must take seriously what you have to accomplish for them. You have to do that with honesty and integrity. Ms. Davis and the Liberty Consulting Services firm take pride in doing just that.

It is not easy in a world that is full companies that will do anything for a dollar by putting people's lives before their money. Ms. Davis says that you must serve in order to be able to lead and that is what she does. Her service is to her God, her family, and her people. When we have our priorities straight we make better choices and decisions. In this day and time it is about helping people to make better choices. As entrepreneurs we are in business for people to patronize us. The more that they are informed the better they feel about the choices that they make. When people feel good about themselves they are better equipped to service others and to serve themselves.

American industry has lost its connection with its customers. In a world of corporate mergers, company executives have disconnected themselves from the average layperson. From the church to the boardrooms, more and more executives have adopted a me, myself, and profits mentality. They care more about making their pockets fatter then they do about the service that their company is providing. Plain and simple corporate America has gotten greedy. I say this not only because of the way that companies are treating their external clients but also how they are treating their internal customers. Companies have cut their employee benefits, as well as salaries, all in the name of business.

You have employees who hate to wake up in the morning just because they have to go to a job that they cannot stand. We have made our employees more disgruntled than ever. We do not give them the courtesy that they deserve nor do we give them the ability to be the best employees that they can be. Corporate executives are so far detached from their employees that they do not know what is needed in order for their company to be successful. When we begin to turn the corner on how we deal with the needs of our employees then we can begin to turn the corner on moving our companies from a chaotic state to a more peaceful environment.

There are some companies that seek to have a corporate environment that is both positive and healthy. They hire consultants to do an evaluation of their corporation from the inside out and try and work on those things that will help to make them a better company. When they pick up the phone to call on such individuals or firms, what they hope to get is someone who will be sincere and trustworthy in the work that they provide. Corporate executives need to know that the consultants they hire will produce quality work. Whether it is putting together a grant proposal or counseling an employee after a tragic event in their life. Companies want consultants who show that they do have a genuine concern for the clients that they deal with. Ms. Davis and Liberty Consulting Services is committed to those that she serves and that does not come easy in an industry that is geared to help others.

THE FUTURE

Respect and honor are two words that are lost from the corporate worlds dictionary. What I have learned from this project is that there are entrepreneurs out here are dedicated to bringing back honor and respect to industries. There are entrepreneurs who are dedicated to doing service right. One of those entrepreneurs who is committed to bringing back respect and honor is Ms. Davis. She is committed to encouraging others and showing them that they can be successful. Helping individuals and corporations gain insight and be able to present a better product or service is what Ms. Davis is all about. She enjoys seeing her clients pleased with the end results when she completes a project or assignment for them. "They may not initially see the benefit when you come in and do training or a proposal but once you are finished and they see the benefit that they are getting out of it and that makes it all worth it", Ms. Davis says.

Taking a chapter from the book of Ms. Oprah Winfrey and her Co-Pastor Suzie Owens, Ms. Davis pushes herself to run a company that will serve its clients, its employees, and its community. She is focused, committed, and disciplined and knows where she wants to take Liberty Consulting Services. She will not stop until she has done a great service for her people and for the overall business community. When you deal with Ms. Davis and Liberty Consulting Services, you will hopefully come away with an encounter that will make you a better person, or company.

Your attitude will have to make an adjustment because of what you have learned about yourself from Ms. Davis and her firm. When you take the tools or talents that you have and use them to better people then you can't help but be successful. Believing in her vision and wanting to be a blessing to those that she helps is what Ms. Davis believes her firm can do now and in the future.

Putting the time and effort into becoming a successful company is something that all entrepreneurs should want to achieve. The way that we do that is by taking our vision and putting it to paper and then bringing it to reality. It makes me feel good to know that there are business owners out there such as Ms. Davis, who long not only to achieve for themselves but also want to be sure that others achieve as well. We in the business world need to understand that we serve to lead and not lead-to-lead. Integrity and passion is being pushed to the side by individuals and corporations. I am glad that there are still a few of us who have not forgotten what those words mean and know how to put them into action.

Talking and doing are two different things. Those who talk may not do and those who do, do not need to talk, because their actions do all the talking for them. I have no doubt that this doer, Ms. Davis; will be affecting the people that she brings on as clients for a long time. The work that she does may seem trivial to some but for those that she enlightens, and empowers, they will be forever changed. She is a woman of integrity, passion, and class. The Mercedes Corporation may have their E-Class, but when you want to affect change in your life, you call on the woman and the company that will do it their way and that is with J-CLASS. There is no other way to do it!

CHAPTER 8

DESIGNING MINISTRY

MELVIN LOWE JR.

PRESIDENT
DESIGNS BY JR and
DEFINING MOMENTS

INTRODUCTION

Hat designer, Melvin Lowe Jr. founded Designs By JR in 1984, inspired by his mother's devoted attire of the Sunday morning hats. He was intrigued by her sense of ownership and outer display of self-dignity, as she accepted heart-warming compliments from her family and friends. Being a witness of these physical, yet emotional interactions, JR began to discover the secret of the lost art of millinery, and its powerful ability to define women.

Best known for his unparalleled knack for innovation and ingenious design of women's chapeaux, JR uses the finest velour felts, glove leather, vintage straw and feathers, as well as unusual materials such as wire, plastics, antique embroidery, mesh, and an array of colored crystal stones. A design by JR collection captures a diverse group of women. It offers contemporary and diverse styles for the independent woman today. Whether seen on television, at a community church, a charity benefit, or an untailored affair, you will be sure to stand out in the crowd. So, pamper yourself like the elite and allow yourself to be dazzled by topping it off with a design by JR.

A couple of years ago I lost my grandmother. My family and I had to go through the process of making the arrangements and handling the ordeal of grieving. My grandmother was a very giving and loving woman with a very funny sense of humor. She had to come here from California for the last six months of her life and we were happy to have her here for that short period of time. During the time that we made the arrangements for my grandmother's funeral we were introduced to a young gentleman that did flower arrangements for such occasions.

When we met with this gentleman he showed us some of his work and we were in awe at what he showed us.

The young entrepreneur gathered our information about my grandmother and other pertinent data that he needed to create this artistic design for her home going service. He took the next few days and brought to life an artistic design nothing short of majestic. When we went to the viewing they opened the doors to the viewing area where my grandmother was lying and our breath was taken away. To say the arrangement was beautiful would not do it justice. The whole ambiance of the room was consumed by this gentlemen's design. Everything from my grandmother's attire, to the color of the casket, to the flower arrangements was perfect. Grandmother was smiling down on us.

I know that funerals are a very sad occasion but there was a warmness in the air that I have never experienced before. From the time that we went in to meet with Mr. Vaughn Greene, the funeral director, who handled getting my grandmother ready for her home going, to the artistic designs created by a young entrepreneur was perfect. Everything was handled with such professionalism and class that my family and I went through the grieving process much easier. When you go through such a traumatic experience of loosing a loved one you need the least amount of chaos.

The warmness and pleasure that my family and I felt in giving my grandmother her proper send off was created by the artistry and design of an entrepreneur who takes each and every artistic creation as an opportunity to bring ministry, joy, and happiness into the lives of the clients that he touches. This young man has done just that with my family and me. Meet the gentleman that takes art and design to heart and sees it as his ministry. Meet Mr. Melvin Lowe Jr. **of Designs By JR and Defining Moments.**

BEGINNINGS

The birthplace of art takes place in the mind. Most artists, whether they are theatrical artists, poetic artists, portrait artists, or designing artists, it all begins in our minds. Our visions can be inspired by any number of things. A verse, a person, an event, a situation, or just life. No matter the inspiration the results remain the same. Every artist wants to bring forth a new creation with each definitive work. Mr. Lowe has been creating these visions for many years. Growing up in Baltimore city is where this young businessman started on his trek to entrepreneurship. Being one of three boys in his family, Mr. Lowe set himself out early to become an entrepreneur. Mr. Lowe says that he knew he wanted to start his own business since high school.

It started with him designing hats for his mother. People learned of his talents and soon started asking him to design hats for them. His mother an entrepreneur herself, gave seed to Mr. Lowe doing the hat designs and the floral designs, which became known as Designs By JR. His business began and people started asking him to do wedding designs, funeral arrangements, and it has grown from there. In the beginning Mr. Lowe says he didn't take his newfound talent seriously because he was unsure of whether or not this was what he wanted to do. He saw that there was inconsistency in the industry that he was about to enter. "You would have your peak time and then it would slow down to the point were there was rarely any work", Mr. Lowe says.

As any beginning entrepreneur should know, when your business first begins there will be periods of ups and downs. What you want to make sure of is that you have more up times then you do down times. The more up times that you have the more cash flow you will have as well. Having steady cash flow in the beginning stages of your business will allow you to be able to do the necessary promotion to gain the name recognition you need. The name of the game in the infancy stages of your business is exposure. The more you have the better your chances of growing.

Mr. Lowe also had a decision to make, and those who have benefited from his artistry are glad that he made the one that he did. He talks about the more he created the hat designs and the floral arrangements, the more creative he became. In the course of his entrepreneurial journey through the designing industry Mr. Lowe has found that there are individuals who do not have your best interest at heart. We have to be careful of the people that we choose as partners and even who we choose as clients.

Everyone does not have the same vision as you and will not see things as you do. Before you choose to go into partnership with someone you need to do your homework. You must make sure that their character, morals, and vision are in line with yours. If not, then you could be headed for disaster. Business owners take risk just being in business. We also take risk with every new project or venture that we embark on. The question is not whether we are up to taking the risk, but can we come out on top of each challenge, and if not how do we get ourselves up for the next one.

Mr. Lowe has shown that he is up to the challenge of being a bright and insightful entrepreneur. Seeing his steady growth and development as an entrepreneur has certainly aided Mr. Lowe to mature and begin to walk his individual path in his industry. As with many of us, when Mr. Lowe first began his business he was not aware of the "business" aspect of being an entrepreneur. As most of us are new to the entrepreneurship level of business, Mr. Lowe had to learn the basics of business when he began his company.

He had to learn how his money worked. He had to learn what he needed to do in order to open a business (commercial) account. He had to learn how to spend his company money wisely. He also had to learn about pricing, mark ups, and vendors. Mr. Lowe talked about how he had to learn where he could buy the best products for his projects. He had to figure how to determine what his time was worth because he was not just providing a product but he was providing a service.

For those up and coming entrepreneurs, you must begin to understand how to calculate what your time is worth. Take a look at what it is that you do and gage how much you should get paid for the time that you put into producing your product. Lawyers and consultants call it "billable hours". It may not be easy to do in the beginning but you can use others that are in your industry to figure what your price point should be.

A price point is the difference between what it cost you to make your product or complete your service and what you actually charge for it. You don't want to set your price too low because you will not make a profit. You do not want to set your price too high because you may lose clients. There is nothing that will cause you to loose customers faster than to make them feel as if they are paying too much for something that is not worth it.

Mr. Lowe talks about how he had to learn the basics of business like how he would determine his mark up. Mark up is the difference between what it costs you to produce a product or service and the price that you actually charge for that product or service. It would cost Mr. Lowe a certain amount of money for the flowers, and various other things for him to create his designs for his hats and his flower arrangements.

He then determined the amount of money that he would charge his clients for that creation. He admits that he had to learn by trial and error at first as we all do but you begin to understand it after a few tries. The last thing that Mr. Lowe talked about trying to understand when he first started was his vendors. Learning where to get certain supplies from can make or break a business. If you are not careful you can run your business right out of business. Again, Mr. Lowe learned about getting supplies through trial and error. He found out that there are some vendors that offer better prices, better service, or a combination of both. The learning comes from being able to determine which company is the best fit for your business.

Mr. Lowe has left those early days of trial and error behind him and has firmly grounded himself in an industry that is growing bigger and bigger for this young entrepreneur.

THE INDUSTRY
Having a clear understanding of this industry is what first intrigued me about this young entrepreneur. He knows his clientele as well as the different dynamics of the industry. Being apart of an industry that can be creatively fulfilling on one hand and challenging on the other is what best describes Mr. Lowe and Designs By JR and Defining Moments are apart of. Mr. Lowe's creativity allows him to bring something fresh and new to each and every client.

No design is the same. Seeing the expression on each clients face gives him fulfillment. Mr. Lowe talked about some of his clients for his hat designs and how some of them come up to him years after he has designed a hat for them and how they are so pleased with his work. He also talks about being in amazement of his own creativity. "Sometimes when I look at some of the designs that I have created, both hats and flower arrangements, I have to take a second look and say, I created that?", he says. Well there are some of us who have experienced Mr. Lowe's creative genius first hand and it is nothing less then breath taking. There is a personal touch to each part of what Mr. Lowe and the Defining Moments and Designs By JR team do.

When Mr. Lowe or his partner Mr. Morgan meets with a client they first seek to get to know their client. By getting to know their client they are able to better understand what they are looking for. There are many in Mr. Lowe's industry that can put an arrangement together, create a hat, or create a décor for an event, but very few can do it with a personal touch, and Mr. Lowe and his company do that well.

Finding out who you are is what helps you to define yourself as well as your business. "If you are going to be successful in any industry you must be focused, and serious about what you do", Mr. Lowe says. Being able to make it through the tough times takes focus and commitment. Every industry has its cycles, and as an entrepreneur you have to be able to navigate through those times.

The more equipped we are the better prepared we are to make it through the tough times. Being successful in this industry comes easy for this entrepreneur because he loves what he does. "That the day that he became happy with who he was is the day that he became happy with what he was doing", Mr. Lowe said. When you have fun at what you do it makes being creative that much easier.

The designing business can be temperamental, there are peak times when things are busy and down times when things are slow. Being diverse in the services that he offers is something that assists Mr. Lowe and his business. The floral designs keeps him the busiest. He has relationships with several funeral homes, which he says keeps him quite busy.

They call him on a consistent basis wanting him to meet with many different families. Partnering with a gentleman by the name of Ted Morgan, has also helped to diversify this young entrepreneur's services. In this modern day and time companies must be able to offer more than just one service. I will say this time after time. People are looking for convenience; they want to be able to buy everything in one place at one time. The more you have to offer to your clients the better your bottom line.

If you want to be at the top of your industry you have to be consistently creative. That means everything that you do has to be innovative. That innovativeness is what drives Mr. Lowe and his business. Being in his creative space is what gives Mr. Lowe his energy. Being able to spend a whole day being creative is what he says he enjoys the most. He is then able to look back at his work and know that he has done something that no one else has. Knowing that you have a mind that is constantly thinking and moving will enable your business to thrive and flourish.

Not being afraid is what will also separate you from others in the design industry or any other industry. This boldness is what started Mr. Lowe into his journey to entrepreneurship as well as the design industry. You have to be willing to put yourself out there in order to be successful at what you do.

If Mr. Lowe was not so bold as to offer his first client an alternative to what she had originally seen then there would not be a Designs By JR or Defining Moments. In many industries you are often pigeon holed to what you can do. This is not so in the design industry. You are free to be as abstract as you want to be. You must be able to think outside the box if you are going to run a successful design business. Mr. Lowe embodies the persona of someone that will not be put into a box and that bodes well for him and his company in the years to come.

THE FUTURE

Just the other day I was reading in the newspaper about a professional football player who was described as the consummate player. The article talked about how this player, who was the quarterback, for one of the better teams in the NFL, studied his opponents on film vigorously. They say that he was someone who backed away from all the fame and stardom that comes with being an NFL quarterback.

This quarterback is one of the younger quarterbacks in the league and has already won 3 super bowl rings. He could easily rest on his laurels and say that he has achieved everything that he has set out to accomplish in his career, but he has not. His work ethic is even more focused now than it ever has been before and he looks to always get better. The way that he has been so successful in his career thus far is because of the amount of time that he spends on his craft. While others may be enjoying the limelight he is busy studying his opponent and working on his technique.

This NFL quarterback has become one of the top 2 quarterbacks in the league because he knows his opponents inside and out. He knows them inside and out because he studies what they do. He knows in certain situations they will do certain things. He has prepared himself for game time situations. Watching him perform on Sunday's is a treat. When you see someone of this quarterbacks stature doing what he does and working as hard as he does it can inspire you to work harder at what you do.

While I was talking with Mr. Lowe I witnessed the same type of passion and determination as the aforementioned football player. He has a focus that will take him and his company well into the future. He studies his clients and gets to know them both inside and out. He takes time to personalize his services for his clients because he feels that adds a special dynamic to the service that he provides. Being in an industry that is dominated by females Mr. Lowe and his business partner have progressed their way into the lives of many who have become their customers.

Being a black man in this industry has had its advantages and disadvantages. As with any young entrepreneur beginning their upward mobility in an industry you have to prove yourself.

People have the expectation that you do not know how to do what it is you say that you can. When they meet with you and begin to listen to you and see that not only you know what you are talking about but also you can go out and produce what you say that you will produce, they start to see you as a professional. Mr. Lowe says, "it gives me great pleasure when I see joy and awe on my clients faces after I have completed a project". "Having people come up to you years after you have completed a project for them and to have them remember you and what you have done for them, puts a smile on my face, says Mr. Lowe".

"When you do things right in business the money will come, says Mr. Lowe". That statement holds true because when you are an entrepreneur like Mr. Lowe, you are about doing things right. When you are about doing things right it also will help you to be a mainstay in your industry because you will have the respect, loyalty and admiration of those who either work for you or are the recipients of your products.

With Mr. Lowe it's not about how he started but it's about helping others in the future. Being able to show that he had compassion for people and just wanted to see them happy. When you give to others it will come back to you. Mr. Lowe, an avid Christian, believes that when you tithe and give to the Lord what he asks of you he will bless you. Whether it is in your business or your personal life, if you will give unto the Lord he will give unto you.

When he talks about tithing and giving, he is not just talking about in the financial sense. "You can tithe by giving your time or your expertise as well", Mr. Lowe says. Designs By J.R. and Defining Moments, is more than just a company, it is a ministry, says Mr. Lowe. The work that he does touches people down in their soul. His clients come away feeling as if they have not just dealt with a business but they have had an encounter with a caring company.

Having a good spirit about where he is and where he is going is present in Mr. Lowe with every word and project that he does. Being able to think like no one else is what will propel this entrepreneur into the future. "The beauty of design is its ability to minister to people", Mr. Lowe says. You never know how an arrangement, a hat or an event that he is apart of will touch someone's life.

With each and every design Mr. Lowe hopes that it will be impactful in someone's life. Mr. Lowe says that he hopes that his hats will make a woman feel like she is somebody. He says that he hopes that his floral arrangements will change someone, that they will see the arrangement and want to start life brand new. His prayer is that with every design, arrangement, and event that he blesses someone. I believe that we are blessed to bless. When we as entrepreneurs realize the power that we have we can have a positive impact on the lives that we touch and our souls can be fulfilled. Mr. Lowe and his company has not only taken the charge to be a blessing but has ministered to those that he has touched, and we are a better people for it.

CHAPTER 9
HOMEBASE

GHILDA WILLIAMS-COLE

SOLE PROPRIETOR
LONG & FOSTER

INTRODUCTION

In this new millennium homeownership has become one of the most important issues on my list. Getting other minorities to embrace that is one of my main focuses as an entrepreneur. My aim with my organization is to enlighten, empower, and invest in the communities that we are part of. When you enlighten someone you teach. When you empower someone, you send them out to use what they have learned. When you invest in someone or something, you give back to them. In this chapter I hope to show the importance of these three things through the power of homeownership.

Homeownership gives individuals access to leverage. When you own a home you gain the potential to build a security that being a renter will not allow. There are millions of individuals who rent apartments or homes for several hundred dollars or several thousands of dollars a month and at the end of the year have nothing to show for it.

I remember riding through a west Baltimore County residence and seeing a house for rent. The house was being rented for $2200 dollars a month. I thought to myself, why would I rent a house for $2200? This to me was beyond my wildest thoughts. I could not imagine paying $2200 and not having anything to show for it at the end of the year. I don't know about any of you but when I see $2200 I know that is what some people pay for a mortgage. I know that if my mortgage was $2200 per month, I would get a tax break the following year for my house. Paying rent is money not used wisely. That is money thrown out the window if you ask me.

We are business owners and we should always think in terms of saving money. I want to see more minority homeownership and I will do my part to show us how to become homeowners. Black Americans only account for 49% of homeownership in this country compared to our white counterparts who account for 76% of homeownership. With such a disparity in the rate of homeownership we must begin to close that gap. In my quest to begin to close the gap. I came across an entrepreneur whose vision and goal was to see more homeowners, and to show individuals how they can make that happen.

This young lady stood out to me because of her strong work ethic and her willingness not only to learn but also to teach others what she has learned. By teaching others what she has learned she has begun to help individuals begin to think about owning a home, that might not otherwise have given it a second thought. This young lady took the franchise route to entrepreneurship and has done it with vigor and intellect. Meet Ms. Ghilda Williams-Coles, sole proprietor of Long & Foster.

BEGINNINGS

This young entrepreneur grew up in the city of Baltimore. Growing up on the East side of Baltimore was where this budding young go getter started on her journey to entrepreneurship. Being the youngest of 3 has its advantages and disadvantages. When you are the youngest in the family you are the one that the older children have to look after. You get away with more and you get the benefit of having your parents be veterans at parenthood by the time you come along. You also take the other side of being the youngest because you are always the last to experience things. Your siblings pick on you because you are the baby in the family and you get all of you brothers or sisters hand me downs.

This young entrepreneur had the task of also growing up with parents who were in the military. For those who have parents in the armed forces it can mean moving from one city after another and you sometimes feel as if you never really get to make friends or develop any foundation. Ms. Williams-Cole found herself on the Eastside of Baltimore and going to school here as well. Once she completed school she received her associates degree in accounting and begin her career trek. Ms. Williams-Cole believes in getting a college education, it does not determine whether or not someone will become an entrepreneur. "Becoming an entrepreneur is determined by ones drive and focus", Ms. Williams-Cole says.

A formal education can help you just as having relative experience and the ability to learn quickly. It all depends on the individual. Ms. Williams-Cole is an avid learner. Her ability to take on a task and learn quickly has helped her in becoming acclimated to an ever changing industry. She is constantly keeping her eyes and ears open to the changes that may effect how she does business. She not only is an avid learner but she is one who takes what she learns and uses that to enhance the service that she gives to her clients.

Being a licensed real estate agent, you have to keep your certifications current and that requires that you obtain a certain amount of class hours. You must also be up to date on the ever changing laws that affect the real estate. Being the shrewd business woman that she is Ms. Williams-Cole makes sure that whatever the requirements are for her to keep up to date in the real estate industry she is doing it.

A hard worker does not even begin to describe the character of Ms. Williams-Cole. She is a woman who did whatever it takes to make things happen. When we talked about beginning her business and getting her real estate license, she worked several jobs just to be able to get through the classes. It was fascinating to me to listen to this young lady say that she worked in a crab house, lifting crates of crabs. Working for a piping company, learning the different types of pipes being used. Looking at this young lady in amazement I thought, "what a focused, and determined woman".

I have the utmost respect for those who are willing to be disciplined enough to achieve the goals that they set for themselves. Ms. Williams-Cole is a woman who will not stop until her goals are achieved, and it shows in her everyday effort to make herself better. You can't help but be captivated by Ms. Williams-Coles beautiful smile and outgoing personality. She is a woman who is not afraid to do and try different things. She is sanguine when it comes to being creative and trying to make things more fecund.

Ms. Williams-Cole has taken her knack for learning quickly and has been focused on building a business that shows people what opportunities that they can have as homeowners. Ms. Williams-Cole talked about when she decided to buy a house there were no agents for buyers, which did not bode well for those who were first time buyers. This ignited her desire to want to become an agent so that individuals would not have to go through the same things that she went through when she purchased her first home. She talks about being at the settlement table and the seller's agent basically telling her to sign a bunch of papers and sent her on her way, "I had no idea what came next", she says.

She did not want anyone else to experience that feeling and has made sure that each of her clients understands what they are signing and what they are getting into when they leave settlement. It is important that people not feel as if they are being taken advantage of when they make one of the most important purchases in their life. Ms. Williams-Cole makes sure that the house that her clients purchase becomes a home because of what they learn through her company.

THE INDUSTRY

There are two different perspectives that we will look at in the real estate industry and Ms. Williams-Cole's company. As I mentioned earlier Ms. Williams-Cole took the franchise route to entrepreneurship. For those of you who do not wish to start a business from the ground up there are always opportunities with a franchise. There are plenty of entrepreneurs who have chosen to use the benefits that come with being a franchisee. Being a franchisee gives you the benefit of an already established name, along with ready made standards and procedures. If you choose to take on a franchise, you will have structure and an already established organization. From a business perspective, a franchise allows you to enter the market much easier than beginning a business from the ground up. You will not have to "get your name out there" when you are a franchise.

I talked with a gentleman just the other day who owned his own franchise for six years, and he talked about how when he began his franchise he already a base of contracts to build off of. He did not have to go right out and search for business because his franchiser had already established his base for him. Now of course the business base did not come free. There is a cost for being a franchise, but we will get into that a little later.

In certain industries, a franchise is done in a different way. In the restaurant business, you may buy a franchise name such as McDonalds, Burger King, or Applebee's. They will set you up with their standards and procedures that you will have to follow. The menus are set in stone and you have a given market that you automatically cater to. You pay them a franchise fee for the use of the name and their business acumen. With a franchise business, you get the safety and security that you do not get when you start your business from the ground up.

In the Hotel industry you can franchise a business as well. In the hotel industry you get the established names such as Choice, Holiday Inn, Hilton, and Marriott. Getting a franchise name is not an easy task either. They take you through a vigorous application process, you must have an ideal location, and you must come to the table with your experience as well as capital. Earvin "Magic" Johnson has done a phenomenal job of using business franchisees to build his corporation. He has taken his name recognition and teamed it with different franchise industries and built an empire that will last long into the future.

There are also franchises that allow you to use their name and business strategies in other industries such as financial planning and real estate. Companies such as State Farm and Long & Foster have been around for years and allow you to become a franchisee with their respective companies. We will talk about the financial planning industry in a later chapter. The real estate industry allows its agents to become independent franchisees by taking their agents through the licensing process and then giving you access to their facilities and established name.

Our current entrepreneur chose the franchise that she became apart of because of its name recognition. Ms. Williams-Cole talked about how when she decided to go into real estate she chose Long & Foster strictly because they were one of the top names in the industry. " I knew what I was getting when I went with Long & Foster". "They had an established name, strong foundation , and good reputation", she says.

Having a good reputation is very important when it comes to being a franchise. People come to know you for that name. Ms. Williams-Cole talked about how being a franchisee can be a double-edged sword. "You get the benefit of the established name and the name recognition, and you also get the draw back of the name", she says. What she explained to me about the drawback of the name is that people don't recognize your business as your business because they see the established franchise instead of you. "Instead of just being Ghilda Williams-Cole, they see you as Long & Foster". "While you are using their name you still are your own company and that can be hard to overcome sometimes", Ms. Williams-Cole says.

When you take on the franchisee tag you must first make sure that what your vision is goes along with the company that you want to become a franchisee with. If your ideals are not the same then you can find yourself constantly butting heads with the franchiser, which is not a good thing. Another draw back to owning a franchise is that you must follow their guidelines. This can keep you from being innovative with marketing, promotions, and the way that you believe that your company should be run. I am a firm believer that not all franchises can be run the exact same way. Each owner has to have their own style of management and how things are run. What you get when you are a franchisee is a cookie cutter type of management system. This is good for some individuals but may not work for others. What you have to decide for yourself is if you want this route to entrepreneurship. Some people feel as if when you are a franchisee you are restricted and in some respect you are. If you are someone who wants to do your own thing then this may not be for you. If it is then you have to understand going into it what you have to do in order to maintain the flag of the franchiser.

When you are a franchisee there are fees that are associated with being a franchisee. Ms. Williams-Cole talked about when she was getting her real estate license Long & Foster required that she pay for different things. She was required to buy a specific calculator that was required by them in order to complete the classes. When I asked her why they could not buy their own calculator she said, "because the calculator that they required you to get did certain things on it that others did not".

They also required that she spend a certain amount of hours in the office in order to take calls. Many franchises have their own guidelines and procedures that you must abide by if you wish to be a franchisee with them and they usually will conduct some type of audit to ensure that you are abiding by those rules. If you do not abide by the guidelines that they stipulate then you will loose your franchise tag and be forced to give up their name.

While franchising in the real estate industry can be quite challenging it also can be a means to obtain wealth. Homeownership is one of the best ways for families to secure their futures. In this day and time it is becoming increasingly imperative that individuals start to think about their futures. Especially those of us in the 20-45 year old age group. Our parents have entered retirement age and will need to be cared for as well as the children that we are raising. We must ensure that we have the means to care for our families both now and in the future. Homeownership is only 49% for black Americans compared to 76% for white Americans.

The disparity in home ownership is becoming more and more evident. The real estate market has just come off one of its best couple of years for sellers. The cost of owning a home has gotten to outrageous proportions. Homes are selling for enormous prices without giving much in return to buyers. We discussed home buying in previous chapters but it is such an important topic for me that I wanted to stress what we need to do in order to close this ever increasing gap in homeownership and finances.

Now some of you may think I am a successful entrepreneur and I have my house and car and this does not pertain to me. If that is the case then fine but there are those who may be just beginning in business or may not yet own a home. For those who do not understand the benefits of homeownership it is crucial that we begin to educate ourselves on this industry. Owning a home could be a way for an individual to get access to capital for your business. The equity in your home can be used to give you the extra money that is needed to start your business or to grow your business. You can also use your home to obtain another home for investment purposes or as a rental property.

These are just a couple of examples of what you can do when you become a homeowner. The options are there for those who want them. The question that you must ask yourself is which one do you choose? Whatever your choice make homeownership your first option. Owning a home and other forms of real estate is also a means to securing not just your future but your families as well. Educating yourself about how you can become a homeowner is one of the best decisions that you could ever make. Once you have decided on becoming a homeowner then you want to make sure that you see individuals such as Ms. Williams-Cole, who will ensure that you get the best value for your dollar. She will treat you as her best friend, as she said to me.

When you are looking to enter into the world of homeownership you want someone that is well educated and knowledgeable of what is going on in the industry. Ms. Williams-Cole is someone who keeps her ear to what is happening in the real estate industry. She and I talk from time to time about what is going on in the industry today. We see the declining trend in the market currently and how it is becoming a buyers market. Sellers are finding it more and more difficult to sell their properties so they are more likely to try to offer incentives to buyers so that they will purchase the property. Sellers have had to drop the price of their properties because they may have been sitting on the market for an extended period of time. Ms. Williams-Cole is an avid learner and is always looking for ways to do things better. This will keep her at the forefront of her industry for years to come. She has developed her own style and persona that separates her from her real estate counter parts.

Ms. Williams-Cole sees the real estate industry entering into a declining trend. The bubble has burst for the industry because of the pricing increase in the market. As a result there are less people willing to pay the prices for houses that sellers are asking these days. Buyers must take advantage of the declining market trend and begin to gain access to homes that might not otherwise be as readily available as they are now.

Ms Williams-Cole talked about how when she first started to look for a home herself there were no agents for buyers and that the industry was basically not looking out for its buyers. Now the industry has agents for both buyers and sellers so that each party can be equally represented. She also says that the industry also has created disclosure forms, which forces sellers to disclose any information that is pertinent to the sale of the home. Ms. Williams-Cole also says that the real estate market has created an environment that will entice more buyers. They have created 35 and in some cases 40 year mortgages. This gives individuals the opportunity to become homeowners that might not other wise be able to purchase a home. The real estate industry is still evolving and those who can keep up with the changing laws and the real estate environment will be the benefactors of it.

For those who are not willing to follow the real estate market and its trends look to entrepreneurs like Ms. Williams-Cole so that you can learn what you need to know and not be taken advantage of when looking into real estate. Ms. Williams-Cole believes being an entrepreneur in the real estate industry gives you more flexibility then other industries. "You can make your schedule to fit your needs as opposed to having to stick to a traditional schedule", she says. "The real estate business is something that you can do anywhere", she says. You do not have to be in one particular area to be in this industry.

She also talked about the disadvantages of being in the real estate business and being a franchise. She says that, you really are not a well known name in the industry. "While you are under the umbrella of a franchise people don't really know who you are. With a franchise you are building there name not yours. "Your hard work goes towards inflating them", she says. She also talked about how since this industry is not a traditional 9 to 5 your clients may want to see a house at all hours and you have to be able to accommodate them. As she says, "you're never off the clock". Being a young entrepreneur in the real estate industry people don't expect you to be as knowledgeable and as young as you are. They tend to think that you are too young and that you do not know what you are talking about. They sometimes look at you in a funny way and sometimes want to ask others to ensure that you know what you are talking about. Getting people to look beyond the young exterior and see you for who you are and what you bring to the table is a constant challenge.

Ms. Williams-Cole is unique in that she has taken on the challenge of entering an industry without the benefit of having someone take her under their wing. She has had to learn about the industry by reading and keeping herself abreast of what is going on in the industry. She has approached the industry with a fearlessness that is not seen in many people these days yet alone in a businesswoman. She does not rest on what she knows about the industry because she knows that it is always changing.

What was relevant 5 years ago may not be relevant today. She prides herself on being able to give others something that she did not have when she became a homeowner. What the business world needs are those individuals such as Ms. Williams-Cole, who are apart of a new breed of business people. Those individuals who care about the well being of others and is willing to show them things that they would not have known had they not encountered someone such as Ms. Williams-Cole. Her industry and the people who will benefit from her expertise will be better off now that they have had an encounter with the Ms. Ghilda Williams-Cole.

THE FUTURE

When you have a genuine love for people and want to see them succeed in life it shows in what you do. That genuineness will show through in how you treat people and how you service them as well. When you put forth the effort to make the service of your clients your first priority then you can do nothing but succeed. Many businessmen and women have not taken seriously the needs of their clients.

They do not seek to make sure that what they are providing is what their customers need. They have placed profits over satisfaction and enlightenment. It is refreshing when you meet entrepreneurs who get that your dissatisfaction is the key to providing good service. You are constantly looking for how you can do business better. Micro-entrepreneurs want to horde over their business. Good entrepreneurs surround themselves with individuals that can get the job done.

Ms. Ghilda Williams-Cole is one of those shrewd entrepreneurs who is constantly striving to do business better with each client. She gains joy in being able to help someone become not just a homeowner but an educated homeowner. She took what she saw was a void in an industry and seeks to fill it on her own. Ms. Williams-Cole seeks to provide a service that people can not only use but can grow from. Being able to offer people financial consulting in respect to how or where to put there money when it comes to real estate is something that she looks forward to being able to offer her clients in the future. Wanting people to understand what is the best way for their money to work for them is important to Ms. Williams-Coles because she wants to see people taking advantage of the opportunities that they are offered in this day and time.

With her outgoing personality and her keen intellect Ms. Williams-Cole and her company is poised to grow in the future. Setting herself apart from others in her industry by doing what many people do not want to take the time and do will keep her flourishing and many people seeking to do business with this young talented entrepreneur. From the first encounter with Ms. Williams-Cole all the way to the settlement table or the follow up call to you about how things are going, you will come away with nothing less than a smile on your face. You will take with you the feeling of calling your best friend up and telling them about this great deal that you just got on a house.

You will not only be pleased with the outcome of the deal that you just made but you will not have the feeling of going into a car dealership and be made to feel that you were just hustled. You will understand what is going on and what else there is to do. You cannot help but feel good about doing service with Ms. Williams-Cole because you know that you are in good company and that she has your best interest at heart. When you do business with Ms. Williams-Cole you know that you are doing business with a consummate professional and some one that will be in your corner no matter what side of the table you are on.

CHAPTER 10
VOLUPTUOUSLY ELEGANT

JENNENE BIGGINS

FOUNDER/CEO
VOLUPTUOUS WOMAN COMPANY
(VWC)

INTRODUCTION

For the past eight years Jennene Biggins, a New Jersey native has served as an advocate for the plus-size community. Although Jennene was not plus size all of her life, as her size began to increase, she became unsatisfied with the choices in fashion that existed for woman with curves and was disgusted by the attitude society exhibits towards plus-size woman.

In November 1997, Jennene founded Voluptuous Woman Company (VWC) based out of Silver Spring, Maryland. The Voluptuous Woman Company's motto "Size is just a Number, Not a limitation.™ " The company serves as a positive voice for the plus-size woman and offers informative, spiritual and empowering events such as networking receptions, conferences, and other special events specifically designed to encourage plus-size woman to live life to the fullest.

The VWC website (www.volupwoman.com) has had over two million visitors to date since its inception in 1998 and serves as an online advocate for today's plus-size woman.

In October 2000, VWC hosted over one hundred woman for a weekend of empowerment workshops, a fashion show and luncheon. Some of Ms. Biggins' accomplish-mints include, publishing the Full Figured Woman's Resource Guide in 1999, conducting a workshop geared towards the plus-size woman at the African-American Woman on Tour Conferences, and working as a freelance writer for Belle Magazine. Ms. Biggins has also been featured in a full-page article in the Washington Times Newspaper in 2000 and in 2003 was featured as the cover in the Washington City Paper.

The year 2003 marked the beginning of a new phase of the VWC. The company began carrying unique clothing and accessories for plus-size woman via their online boutique. In 2005, Ms. Biggins and the VWC were chosen as one of eight companies to accompany the U.S. Department of Commerce Office of Textiles and Apparel on a Plus-Size Apparel and Accessory Trade Mission to London, England and Dusseldorf, Germany.

In July 2005, VWC launched their premier apparel product - Voluptuous Bath Wraps (www.Plussizebathwraps.com).
The Voluptuous Bath Wrap was designed specifically for the plus-size woman who experienced the "shortcomings" of the average bath towel. The bath wrap is made of 100% luxurious terry cotton velour and fits curvy woman size 14-30. The bath wraps will be carried by day spas, boutiques and hotels throughout the United States and internationally.

Ms. Biggins resides in Forestville, Maryland and is a member of Union Temple Baptist Church were she serves as Chairperson of the Entrepreneur Ministry and serves on the Ministry Vision Team, which oversees all church ministries.

In this new era of womanism, a new standard is being set. Women of today are becoming more and more comfortable and confident in themselves, especially those of the voluptuous size. They are embracing who they are and are not afraid of being sexy. They are becoming more and more comfortable in their own skin and allowing everyone around them to know that they love who they have become.

In this country what is seen and constantly shoved in our faces are woman who are less than a size 6. Well, if America's idea of sexy is a size 6 then that maybe fine for them but you cannot force others to like what you like and believe what you believe. You cannot force others to believe that your standard of beauty should be everyone else's.

As you watch the music videos, look at the magazine ads, or watch television commercials, you are pushed to believe that only super model type woman are sexy. Well, there is a new standard being set in our society in this modern 21st century. The plus size women are no longer sitting on the sidelines and being silent. They are standing up and putting other woman on notice. They are letting them know that we can be sexy and sassy too!

They are no longer accepting the dull and mundane clothing lines that use to be put on the market for the plus size woman. They are forcing the fashion industry to listen to what their demands are and are forcing them to cater to their needs. With comedian Monique standing front and center as a sexy and sassy plus size woman, she is showing women in a major way that you are beautiful no matter what size you are.

Because of woman like Moni'que the fashion and movie industry are starting to recognize that the voluptuous woman has a voice too. Statistics have shown that in our country today, the average size of a woman is a size 14 . With that being said there must be a change in how we perceive the women of today. Some industries are slowly beginning to see that the plus size woman has a voice in the products they offer.

The voluptuous woman is taking her place in society and industries are beginning to listen to what they have to say. In my travels, I have come to find a woman who has found her voice in the world of fashion and design. She is someone who has also taken on the mantle for the plus size woman and is blazing the trail for those women that were thought to be silent. She is someone who has an inner exuberance that will engulf you and welcome you into the world that is hers. She exudes confidence and her intellect is second to none.

They say that necessity is the mother of invention. When this young entrepreneur saw that the women of her status were not being accommodated she set out to ensure that they would be catered to like everyone else. She was dissatisfied with what she saw in the fashion industry and sought to publicize that there would be a new voice in the business of fashion. The voluptuous woman would no longer accept the tired old fashions that were being created. They wanted to look as sexy and be as sassy as any other woman. Well, thanks to this young entrepreneur the fashion and bath wrap industry will no longer be the same. It will no longer be acceptable for plus size women to stand on the sidelines and not have what they want.

This young entrepreneur is a trailblazer, is taking her industry by storm and is not afraid of pushing it to the next level. The standard is being set for the plus size women. She is not only feeling good on the inside but also looking good on the outside. In this day and time women are not afraid of letting their woman ness be known. That I believe is in part due to the sassy sexy, voluptuous women like Ms. Jennene Biggins of the **Voluptuous Woman Company**, the entrepreneur who is creating a new style that I call "voluptuous elegance", in the fashion world and giving the plus size woman there voice.

BEGINNINGS

The state of New Jersey is where this young woman of distinction began her journey to entrepreneurship. Being brought up with a catholic school education both in middle and high school her talents were numerous. She was an avid piano player, senior class president, and all around activity buff. As she says, "I was always involved in something". She attended college at Howard University, where she majored in Business Administration. She graduated with her degree in business and did various other jobs before starting her Voluptuous Woman Company in 1997. Some of her jobs included working in the Hotel and Restaurant Management field for several years and also doing some event planning.

Ms. Biggins says that she has always had the entrepreneurial spirit and as she concluded her educational sabbatical, she would get the spark that would transform her from an everyday line level worker to a young and inspired business leader. Ms. Biggins says that she was always a woman who loved fashion. She took pride in how she dressed and carried herself. She says that a co-worker of hers made a comment one day about her dressing well for someone her size and Ms. Biggins says that she did not know how to take that comment. She then thought to herself that she would take a negative stereotype and turn it into a positive one about plus size women.

For many years voluptuous woman have not always been seen in a positive light. They have been made to feel as if they had no taste for fashion and that what they wanted to wear did not count. Ms. Biggins took this misnomer and was determined to show people not only in the fashion world but people in general that the voluptuous woman had a voice and would be heard.

114

Ms. Biggins says that she was not always a plus-size woman and when she began to look for clothes that would fit her; she was dissatisfied with what was offered for woman of her status. Ms. Biggins, in 1997 hosted her first networking Reception and Fashion show. From there the Voluptuous Woman Company (VWC) has not looked back. Wanting to stop making other people rich also was the driving force behind Ms. Biggins wanting to pursue her dream of owning her own business.

Perceptions can be misleading if you ask me. People have, for many years expected less from Black-Owned and Black Operated businesses. Well, Ms. Biggins and the VWC are tearing down those walls of misperceptions. "Giving my clients quality service is her main priority", says Ms. Biggins. While Ms. Biggins does not believe that the customer is always right, she does believe that you must do what is necessary to provide the service that they deserve. Providing good service is the backbone to any business and if you cannot give good customer service then you will not be in business for very long. Ms. Biggins and the VWC have found a way to give good service and keep her customers constantly satisfied. The better your customer service the more people will want to do business with you. When you can be professional and courteous to individuals they will not only want your product or service, they will tell others about it.

What Ms. Biggins has created with VWC is a company that caters to woman and makes them feel good about themselves. This is evident in her slogan "Size is just a number, not a limitation". When women come to a VWC event they will hopefully come away with a feeling of empowerment, enlightenment, and encouragement. They will hopefully understand that there is more to them then just their size. Being a full and complete woman from the inside out is what more and more women are starting to realize nowadays.

They are realizing that their self-esteem must come from within. When you carry yourself with confidence those who encounter you will have no choice but to be taken in by how you feel about yourself. In this day and time it is imperative that both men and women learn to believe in themselves. The more confident that we are in ourselves and our abilities then the more successful we will be. Ms. Biggins is doing her part to ensure that women of today carry themselves in a manner that is respectable, elegant, and confident. Women of today are accomplishing great things and the voluptuous woman is building that confidence more and more with individuals such as Ms. Biggins.

With her networking events and fashion shows Ms. Biggins has empowered plus size women all over the country. Ms. Biggins and VWC have begun a movement. I recall watching an interview with Tavis Smiley and he was talking about his book the Covenant with Black America. The host was asking him about the movement that is being created by his book and how it is affecting change in the black community. His response was that the book has different levels.

To paraphrase, he said that the first level of the book was the thought process; the second level was the momentum of the book, and the third level being a movement. Ms. Biggins has taken the plus size industry and opened many people's minds about voluptuous women; she is creating a momentum that will keep getting bigger, and will help progress the movement and show others that the plus size industry is a viable stream of income.

Ms. Biggins is turning the plus size industry upside down with her exuberance and tenacity and giving notice to industry doubters and haters. She is showing women no matter what their size that you can be anything that you set your mind to. You can be as successful and as elegant as you want to be no matter what others may say or think about you.

THE INDUSTRY

There is a paradigm shift going on in America. The re-imaging of America is beginning. More and more women are realizing that the images that are portrayed on television and in magazines is not the average American woman. They are seeing themselves for who they are as women of character and substance, not just women of body and beauty. The plus size industry is beginning to turn the corner as a viable income stream for fashion today.

This was not so when Ms. Biggins first started her company. She says, "the plus size industry was very low key, and there were very few stores for plus size women to shop". You had very few designers that catered to the plus size woman and women were not comfortable enough with themselves to shop for clothing that fit them. Women, "back in the day", who were plus size, did not have the choices that they now have.

Many retail stores as well as industry designers are realizing that the average size woman in America is not a size 6 but a size 14. As they are coming to this realization they are beginning to change the way that they see voluptuous women. Not only are industry people beginning to see this but many women are beginning to see it as well. "They are no longer easily manipulated into believing that you have to be a size 6 in order to be healthy", says Ms. Biggins.

Some women believe that you can be a plus size woman and be healthy. What Ms. Biggins and her organization are doing is setting a standard in her industry. She is showing women that you can be intelligent, elegant, classy, sexy, and voluptuous. Her desire and energy for what she does is infectious. When you are in Ms. Biggins presence you see a confident businesswoman who will stop at nothing to be successful, and will take many women along with her for the ride.

The VWC and Ms. Biggins have created a stage that will put the voluptuous woman front and center. "People must understand that we are not the same color, size, or height. Society has this box that they want to put us in", Ms. Biggins says. There are woman such as Moni'que, Queen Latifah, and Ms. Biggins, who refuse to allow society to put them in a box.

They are showing that it is ok to be comfortable with being a plus size woman. They are showing millions of women today that you are the only one who puts limitations on you. The plus size industry is getting more comfortable with themselves. They are seeing more and more positive images of themselves in television, and magazines. There were not many magazines available that catered to plus size women's fashion but they are now opening those doors and seeing that the plus size market is on the rise and creating a believer out of those who said that the plus size market does not matter.

The mainstream manufacturers and designers are realizing that the plus size market is growing. As I mentioned before Ms.

Biggins said that the average size woman is a size 14, which means that mainstream designers now have to consider designing their clothing for women who are voluptuous. This shift in the industry is creating new revenue streams for manufacturers and traditional designers so they see the benefit in catering to this untapped market. As any good businessman or woman knows, the more diverse your market the better your bottom-line. Ms. Biggins talked about the effect that the plus size industry is having on television and cable. She talked to me about how the comedian Moni'que pitched her show "Big Fat Chance" to several different networks before it was picked up on the Oxygen network.

It was the highest rated show on the network. The oxygen network is not carried on all local Comcast cable networks, which gave it a limited viewing audience. Ms. Biggins says that it would have been able to reach an even wider audience if it was carried on the Comcast cable national network. In the television world just as with many other industries, those who run the major companies do not want to get on board with something new until it is successful. They don't want to take the risk.

Well, Ms. Biggins and the rest of the VWC family are taking that risk and running with it. They are showing businesses in the industry that success is what you can achieve when you listen to what your heart tells you. Ms. Biggins is seeing the buying power that plus size women have and is listening to that voice. The buying power is getting stronger and Ms. Biggins believes that it will be more powerful than ever within the next five years. The increase in internet technology is allowing Ms. Biggins to reach women all over the world. She sees the plus size market as an untapped market due to the vastness of the internet. The internet gives you access to people that you traditionally would not be able to reach.

Ms. Biggins adds a personal touch to her business that not many others in this industry do. She says, "My business is my ministry". So many people, no matter what industry they are in do not bring or want to bring God into the workplace, but Ms. Biggins believes that a positive word in someone's life can go a long way. Not being afraid to listen to what others have to say can help you enhance your business. As an entrepreneur you have to be willing to live outside the box.

Being passionate about what you do will drive you to where you want to go. With her passion and her determination Ms. Biggins is giving the voluptuous women the strength to stand up and feel confident in herself. She is not only doing it for the plus size woman she is doing it for women in general.

THE FUTURE

America is supposed to be a progressive society. There are some industries that are experiencing a tremendous amount of growth such as the oil industry, the health care industry, and the technology industry. The hospitality industry went through its growth spurt during the mid to late 90's, while the real estate industry is just coming out of its growth spurt over the past couple of years. There are those industries that are at the brink of experiencing growth and advancement.

The publishing industry is one of those industries and the other is the plus size industry. What these two industries have discovered is something that is very similar. The publishing industry has discovered something that we in the black community have known for a long time, that there are some talented writers in our midst.

They have seen that there is a new market that has yet to be tapped and they are trying to find ways to capitalize on this new market called "urban fiction". While there are black authors who are stepping up and coming to the forefront of the publishing industry, we are still not getting our fair share of the market place nor are we seeing an increase in publishing companies.

Hopefully, I will be changing that in the years to come. The same issue exists in the plus size industry. The industry is now beginning to see the growth in this particular market and are trying to capitalize on this new market. Mainstream industry goers are seeing the money that has not been tapped in this industry. They are beginning to see the market demand that the plus size industry has created. There is also the demand for more black ownership in the plus size industry and with phenomenal women like Ms. Biggins; an explosion is about to happen in the industry. The plus size industry is gaining its wings and is on the incline. Ms. Biggins has gained her wings and is looking forward to the future.

The VWC and Ms. Biggins have entered the future by launching their new Voluptuous Bath Wrap line. This line was specifically designed for the plus size woman. It was the vision of Ms. Biggins, who saw the shortcomings of the average bath towel, so she decided to create a bath wrap that would give the plus size woman what she desired in a bath wrap. They are also using the internet to expand and reach a broader market.

Ms. Biggins sees the growth potential in using the internet as a means to reach her target market. She says, "the internet has provided VWC with more clients than ever before". As Ms. Biggins and VWC look into the future they are approaching it with tenacity and vigor that other entrepreneurs seek to have. Bringing out the passion that is within her has not been a problem for this young entrepreneur. She has been adamant about educating others on this industry and its potential and helping others know what she has known for years. Her spiritual soundness has taken her thus far and will take her a long way in the future.

Education and wisdom is the key to advancement. No matter the industry the more you know about that industry the better off you will be and the industry as a whole. Young entrepreneurs can take note of what Ms. Biggins has done to take this generation of entrepreneurs from a talking generation to a doing generation. She not only talks about business but is handling her business when it comes to the plus size industry. She is hard working, tenacious, determined and loves the Lord. She has introduced to many the new voice in the fashion industry and that voice is sexy, sassy, classy, elegant and most of all Voluptuous!

CHAPTER 11
SERVICE ON THE GO

SCOTT NEWELL

PRESIDENT/OWNER
TIRES ON THE GO INC.

INTRODUCTION

This is by far the most interesting entrepreneur that I had the pleasure to talk with in this book. In this modern day of hustle and bustle, we find ourselves running here, going there, and not enough time to do anything that we planned to do. Between working a 10-hour day, running the kids to rehearsal or some kind of practice, we don't have time to do the little things that we have to get done.

The house goes unclean, the laundry gets backed up, and the refrigerator is a forgotten utility. We live at the fast food chains, and just like at cheers everybody knows our name. We use the microwave to the extent that our ovens have plotted their demise, while Sunday dinners at "Big Mama's is a long forgotten tradition. While we long for rest and relaxation we cannot even begin to enjoy what little peace and relaxation that we may have at the end of our days.

The older generation has found it harder to enjoy their golden years because they have had to work beyond their retirement years. They have had to become parents all over again and have been forced to deal with still being a part of the everyday turmoil of the workforce. They have earned the right to enjoy their latter years but because of the instability of our country's economy they have been forced to subsidize their income. The social security that they worked so hard to earn has been wiped away just by the stroke of a pen of our government. They are playing games with what the baby boomers have worked so hard to obtain.

The next generation has totally lost the sense of labor and effort. We want everything now and in a hurry. We think that everything should be given to us and not earned. We have become so lazy in our thinking that we shop from home and expect it to be delivered to us at our front door. There are some industries that have seen this shift in our society and are beginning to adhere to the calling.

When I worked in the hospitality industry there were a few hotel chains that saw the need of convenience. They saw that people were moving to a one-stop shop ideology. People wanted to be able to go to a hotel and get everything that they needed right in their room or in the hotel. In the retail industry some retailers have realized that their customers wanted to be able to come to their store and buy everything they needed. Wal-mart saw this, Men's Wearhouse saw this, and many other businesses are beginning to see that our customers want to shop conveniently. We have less time to do things so we want to be able to get everything that we can in one place.

Well, in my travels I met an entrepreneur who took heed to what customers wanted. He saw that our society was moving in a direction that was trying to meet people where they were. He saw a unique opportunity that no one else in the industry saw. When I first spoke with this young and gifted entrepreneur and he told me what he did I could not do anything but think to myself that this idea was nothing short of brilliant. The service that he provided was nothing new but the concept in which he delivers it was unique. People on a daily basis get their cars serviced. They take time off from work to get routine car maintenance, and even take time off when those unforeseen circumstances occur. I have learned the hard way the importance of taking care of my truck.

Keeping it in good running condition is more than one of my top priorities. My truck is my lifeline to everything that I do. It is how I get to work to make the money that helps me earn a living. Without it I am hard pressed to do the things that I need to do. There are many who use our public transportation systems to get here and there, but for me I like the convenience of being able to go outside, slide into my truck, turn my music on and ride!

There is someone who makes sure that we are able to get in our cars, trucks, and SUV's and ride. In this day and time we don't have time to take our cars in to be serviced so meet the young man that will bring the service to you. He is Mr. Scott Newell of **Tires On The Go**. He will ensure that whether you are riding on 14's or 22's, or sliding into your Jeep Grand Cherokee, or your Bentley, that your ride is secure as you go where you need to be.

BEGINNINGS

This Boogie Down Bronx native made his way to Maryland when he was still in his developmental years. Using the county school system as his backdrop for his education Scott went on to enter Lincoln University. After spending two years at Lincoln Mr. Newell decided that the pursuit for higher learning was not the path that he wanted to take. Being the visionary that he was he decided to take the ideas that he had and put them to use. Believing that one does not have to have a college degree in order to be a successful entrepreneur he went on to bigger and better things.

Mr. Newell's out the box thinking helped him to believe in his talents and his abilities that he would develop along his entrepreneurship journey. Not wanting to be pigeon holed into what some of us believe about college, Mr. Newell knew that he would not be one who would work for someone else for very long. There are some of us who feel that we never fit into what mainstream society teaches us. Go to school so that you can get a good education, so you can get a good job, and live a good life. There are some of us who believe that a good education helps in your development but that education along with common sense can help you in developing your own business and have others working for you.

College campuses are filled with young minds that are shaped and molded into believing that working for someone else is the safe thing to do. Well, entrepreneurs like Mr. Newell do not believe in being safe. Going out and pursuing your vision is what some of us must do. Our creative mindset will not allow us to see things as others do. There are those like Mr. Newell, who have so many ideas inside of them that working for someone else would be like taking a wild animal and trying to raise them in a caged environment. They will feel out of place and will not be able to be who they were created to be.

The environment is not conducive to what they are used to so it creates an unhealthy place for the individual. Entrepreneurs are a unique breed of people. Most of us do not think like others and we do not see things as others do. This is the case that I not only found in the other entrepreneurs that are a part of this book but also in Mr. Newell. Most business concepts are cookie cutter concepts. There is not much that has not been done when it comes to most industries.

What most businessmen and women must figure out when they start their own business is how to do it better than others. Well, this was the case with Mr. Newell and Tires On The Go Inc. Mr. Newell talks about when he was working for an auto repair store and seeing the number of customers that were dissatisfied with the service that they received. He says, "they would complain about the amount of time that they would have to wait in order to get their car serviced". He came up with the idea from that bit of information that customers gave him. Having the customers upset and yelling about being there for 1 or 2 hours sparked him to develop the concept that would become Tires On The Go.

From its inception Tires On The Go was created with the client who is busy and always on the go. For those individuals who do not have time to spend at the repair shop, Mr. Newell will bring the shop to you. Mr. Newell does make an appointment with you to service your car. You can buy tires from him that you would buy from Sears, Merchants or Goodyear. He will come to your place of employment or your residence and change and balance your tires. He also does minor car maintenance. So while you are at work you can have your car serviced or while you are at home you can have your car's taken care of.

This reduces time that you would have to spend to take your car to a mechanic. Our time is one of the most valuable assets that we have and we must use it to the fullest. Mr. Newell saw how much people disliked having to take their cars into the mechanic and waiting 2 or 3 hours to get it serviced and as a result developed a business that would come to you. You cannot imagine the number of people who would like to eliminate the hassle of having to take their car into the shop to be serviced.

Mr. Newell's service is not for everyone. Those who do not see the value in the service that he offers do not understand what customer service is all about. How many other businesses will come to your door and give you a product or service, other than the shopping network. What Mr. Newell offers is much better than any shopping network and worth the time that you will save by using Mr. Newell's services. What others in his industry may offer to you is countless hours waiting on mechanics that are only looking to increase their bottom line. What Mr. Newell wanted to offer to people was a way that they could get their cars serviced and save time.

After spending time working for someone else and having a burning desire getting stronger inside of him, Mr. Newell felt that he could offer to his clients what the others in his industry were not giving to them. He simply found his niche and brought to an old industry a new means of offering people a way to keep going while their car gets serviced. For most of us our cars are just like children. We must take the time to make sure that they have the proper maintenance just as a child needs proper nurturing. Cars, just like children, will break down if you do not have the proper up keep. Routine maintenance on your vehicle will allow you to be able to keep your car for many years. In a day and time when people's finances are at a minimum, the better you take care of your car the fewer headaches you will have, and Mr. Newell offers that to those who see his value.

THE INDUSTRY

One thing that any owner of a car knows for sure is that they will have to get it serviced at one point in time. It does not matter who you are you will have to get your oil changed; tires changed, or get a tune up. The question is where do you go to get it done and how much time will you have to spend doing it. I had a friend of mine who only goes to the dealership to get her car serviced and she spends several hours waiting for them to finish with her car. Every time I talk to her after she has been to the dealership to she is always upset and frustrated about the amount of time that she has to spend at the dealership.

Not only does she have to be frustrated about the amount of time that it takes them to service her car she also has to deal with the outrageous prices that they charge for servicing her car. I ask

125

her all the time why she goes to the dealer and she says because it is the only place that she feels comfortable having her car looked at. I tell her that she may feel comfortable going there but the price that she pays in time and in money is ridiculous! I believe that you can get the same quality service for your car from other mechanics for a fraction of the price and time.

There are a few people that you always need to have in your life and a good mechanic is one of them. Having someone that you can trust with the care and maintenance of your car is invaluable. I remember growing up my mom having a couple of cars and she would always take them to our Uncle Benny when she needed to have work done. He taught her the importance of doing routine maintenance on your car and to always make sure that you do your oil changes. Well, she in turn has passed that down to me. Even though I have had my issues with cars I have always kept that lesson deep in my heart.

My mother, my sisters and I laugh about the cars that my mother had but the one thing that we never had to worry about was those cars breaking down or if they did or who she would take them to. Even now as we are older I still remember the lesson that my mother taught me about having one good mechanic to take care of your car. When you are entrusting your car care to a business or an individual you must make sure that you do your homework on that individual or that company.

Do not take for granted that everyone has your best interest at heart. There are predatory mechanics out here that will try and take advantage of you, especially if you are a woman. You must be careful that the company that you deal with is sincere and will have your best interest at heart. Your life may depend on it! You must develop a friendship with a good mechanic and one person that I believe has his clients best care at heart is Mr. Scott Newell.

His desire to see his clients riding in a vehicle that is as trouble free as possible stands out from the rest of those in the industry. He wants to see people save time and be convenient at the same time. He is as accommodating, as his clients need him to be and more flexible than anyone in his industry. Then again, that is why his business is named what it is, Tires On The Go Inc.

The tire and car repair industry has gone through its share of changes but the one thing that people want the most is convenience, says Mr. Newell, and people are willing to pay for it. Even with the price of tires increasing and the increase of oil, people still are willing to pay for convenience. What Mr. Newell has created is a unique industry for himself.

When he talked about what he does and others who do similar work, there is no one that does what he does and how he does it. There is no other company in Virginia that will give you the service that Mr. Newell and Tires On The Go Inc. gives you. You cannot find anyone who will come to your house or your place of business and perform tire replacement, balancing, and oil changes. The one thing that Mr. Newell says that people have grown to want more since he first started in this industry is convenience.

He says that people have grown more and more convenience. "People don't want to deal with issues that have to do with getting their cars repaired", says Mr. Newell. "They just want what is wrong to be fixed", says Mr. Newell. I believe that people have become so busy that they now look for companies and businesses that will make things as convenient as possible for them. This is the backdrop for what gave Mr. Newell his innovative idea of bringing the service to his customers.

People have seen the uniqueness in what Mr. Newell does, especially on the commercial side of his business. He has both commercial and residential clients that love the fact that they do not have to take their cars or trucks into a shop to be serviced. By doing tire replacement, balancing, and minor car repair Mr. Newell and Tires On The Go sets itself apart from others who are now catching on to what Mr. Newell saw several years ago. People's idea of service and convenience are steadily changing and it is entrepreneurs like Mr. Newell who are on the front side of the bell curve that are filling the peoples need for convenience.

There are those who are not afraid to think outside the box when it comes to business and Mr. Newell is certainly one of those people. In a day and time when people's patience is very thin when it comes to service it's companies like Tires On The Go that

127

help individuals and companies rest a little easier when it comes to taking care of their vehicles.

THE FUTURE

Mr. Newell and Tires On The Go are steadily growing. More and more people are seeing the value in getting your car serviced while you are at work or at home. Businesses that have transportation vehicles are also seeing the benefit of not having to take their trucks into the shop. Tires can be changed, rotated, or fixed right their outside your business while your other vehicles are out doing what they need to do. As more and more companies catch onto what Mr. Newell is doing they will try to mimic what he has done.

They may take his concept and build off of that but what they will not be able to grasp is his innovative spirit and strong desire to think different. The one thing that you will get with Mr. Newell and Tires On The Go Inc. is something different. Seeing what has been created by Mr. Newell is something that I myself am awed by. To sit and listen to his desire to not be like anyone else is infectious. Having a keen interest in what people want will go a long way in any industry and Mr. Newell has made sure that Tires On The Go Inc. is one of those companies.

Moving forward is something that every entrepreneur does with their business. Mr. Newell is no exception. Being diverse in the services that he offers to his clients is something that will continue to propel him into the future. Opening up his business to an even broader customer base will only increase the visibility of this creative business design. The businesses that are on the cusp of what Mr. Newell does can only marvel at where he is taking Tires On The Go Inc.

Being creative and using common sense has helped this young entrepreneur to believe that when you offer people a service that exceeds their expectation and gives them the convenience that they want will only lead to more people demanding what you have to offer. Being structured is not one thing that Mr. Newell is going to be and when others in his business follow his out the box tactics to give customer satisfaction they can only hope to be as successful as he is.

The thing that Mr. Newell's customers can appreciate about his company is that with his preventive maintenance his customers can also find out if there is something that will need to be fixed in the near future. His clients appreciate that he is not trying to sell them something that they do not need. Since he does not do major maintenance work he can let them know what needs to be fixed and how much time they have to fix it.

Even with the fluctuation in the oil and tire market Mr. Newell finds a way to keep his prices competitive. In this ever changing economy and markets that we as entrepreneurs deal with we have to always be looking for ways to stay ahead of the game. Its good to know that Mr. Newell and Tires On The Go Inc. keep their customers first and always want to make sure that when your cruzin in your ride that your riding with Tires On The Go!

CHAPTER 12
THE KING OF TRANSPORTATION

ALLAN TAYLOR

PRESIDENT/CEO
TAYLOR MADE TRANSPORTATION

INTRODUCTION

This is a small world that we live in. When I was doing my profile on Mr. Scott Newell from Tires On The Go Inc. he mentioned that he had a friend that owned his own business as well. He mentioned the young entrepreneurs name to me and at the time I did not think anything of it. Then once we went through the profiling process we discussed his friend again. I added him to my list of entrepreneurs to possibly profile and have as a part of this book. During our conversation Mr. Newell also mentioned what a great friend this entrepreneur was and how inspirational he was to him. He started to mention a couple of things about his friend and one of the things that he mentioned was that he attended the University of Maryland Eastern Shore. This peaked my interest because it was also the school that I graduated from.

As I started to think about Mr. Newell's friend's name it sparked my memory of a classmate that I had. I then asked Mr. Newell if his friend was a Hotel and Restaurant Management major at UMES. He responded, "Yes, he believed so". I then went on to tell Mr. Newell of the classmate that I had who had the same name as his friend.

Mr. Newell then quickly called his friend up and asked if he knew a young man by the name of Leroy McKenzie (me) and he said yeah, we were in the same major together at UMES. Mr. Newell then went on to tell the other young entrepreneur that I was doing the profile on him and was interested in doing the same on him. I then got on the phone with the young entrepreneur and talked about how each of us had been doing since school. This world we live in is a small funny place. Well, needless to say that young entrepreneur and I got together and talked a little business and talked about the good old days. Meet Mr. Allen Taylor of **Taylor Made Transportation.**

<u>BEGINNINGS</u>

This Baltimore native was a product of the parochial school system. Attending catholic school from kindergarten through the 12th grade was the start to this entrepreneur's path of education. Attending one of the premier catholic high schools in the Baltimore area, Cardinal Gibbons, Mr. Taylor learned those core values that he still adheres to today.

Those of us who grew up in Baltimore know the value of having a good education and individuals that helped to push you to pursue excellence. Once graduating from high school Mr. Taylor attended the University of Maryland Eastern Shore, where he would graduate with a Bachelors Degree in Hotel/Restaurant Management.

Once Mr. Taylor left school he entered into the Hotel / Restaurant industry and would find that it was not to his liking so he went back to school to pursue further education at Morgan State University. He would get his Masters degree from Morgan in Transportation and Logistics Management. Mr. Taylor says that when he left the hospitality industry he wanted to become an air traffic controller until they were laid off. He had an individual who suggested that he attend school for Transportation/Logistics Management and that's what he did.

While he attended Morgan State University he was bitten by the entrepreneur bug. He did an internship at the Motor Vehicle Administration and then with Intelligent Transportation Society of America (ITS), located in Washington D.C. By the time he finished his master's degree at Morgan State he was eager to get started on his career with ITS America. They unfortunately had other plans and would not see the same vision that Mr. Taylor had for himself with their company.

God has a way of taking those things that were meant for evil and turning them around and using them for good. When Mr. Taylor was not offered a position with ITS America he did not drop his head and sulk but decided that he would use his talents to build his business instead of helping someone else build their business. That was the beginning of Taylor Made

132

Transportation. In July of 1996 Mr. Taylor opened the doors of Taylor Made Transportation and has not looked back since.

Believing in the educational background that he had Mr. Taylor says that college helped to prepare him become an entrepreneur. He says that while college prepares you to work for corporate America it does not stress entrepreneurship enough. A college education gives you the ability to open your mind and to make certain contacts. Mr. Taylor says that college taught him how to read contracts, how to write well, and how to communicate well. He says that these three essential tools are the key to being successful in any business at any level.

Mr. Taylor also says that college teaches you how to deal with certain rejections but there is nothing like real life experiences to help one get an understanding of how to deal with many types of individuals. He believes that to be a successful entrepreneur you have to be able to deal with different types of people. "You have to be able to deal with someone who may only have a 4th grade education as well as deal with someone who has a Harvard education, says Mr. Taylor". I believe the better you are at navigating between the two the better off you will be. When you are an entrepreneur you have to know that you will have to communicate with people and be able to communicate with them in such a way that they will be able to understand you as well as you understand them.

Being able to communicate clearly and distinctly will aid you in being able to meet and exceed the expectations of your customers, which is how Mr. Taylor defines customer service. Doing the little things can go along way in any business. Speaking to customers when they enter your establishment, treating them with respect, and courtesy, are just a few things that Mr. Taylor believes that you must do in order to meet and exceed the expectations of your customers.

If you can meet and exceed the expectations of your customers they will come back to you over and over again and they may even lead you to other businesses. Finding a way to meet and exceed the expectations of your customers can be stressful. Finding ways to do that amidst dealing with employee issues, management issues, vendor issues, family issues, and personal issues, can be quite a challenge and a disadvantage to being an entrepreneur, says Mr. Taylor.

Being the boss means that you have to be able to deal with everyone's issues and still get the job done. Mr. Taylor says, "that people do business with people because they know individuals". When things happen the people will look to you to find out what happened not your employees. Your employees may come and go and you have to still get things done. Those entrepreneurs who get things done in spite of all of the adversities are the ones that are successful at what they do.

The entrepreneur who does not put his head down every time something goes wrong is the one who at the end of the day will see that the advantages far out way the disadvantages to being a young and gifted entrepreneur. Mr. Taylor has proven that he is one of those individuals and Taylor Made Transportation is a business firmly grounded in getting things done.

THE INDUSTRY

" I challenge you to name an industry that does not involve transportation". These were the words of Mr. Taylor to me when we were talking about his business and his industry. Mr. Taylor told me every industry and individual needs some form of transportation. We need it to get to work, to go to the store, to get anything that we need, to get somewhere we need some form of transportation, even if it's to the moon. Taylor Made Transportation is built to give that to you and more. Ever since the invention of the motor vehicle we have increased the ways in which we get from one place to another. What has been the challenge from inception is making the ability to get from one place to the other faster. Transportation is a part of our everyday life.

We can't function without it. Whether you work on land or sea you need to be able to get from one place to the other. The question is when you think transportation who do you think of? Well, Mr. Taylor wants your first thought to be Taylor Made Transportation, and where this young entrepreneur and his transportation company is headed it will be.

For minorities the transportation industry just as any other industry is very difficult to enter. The old adage is that we have to work twice as hard to be just as good. In the transportation industry it is no different. Making a mark in your industry is challenging enough but that challenge is even greater when you are a minority owned business. Your company is expected to be flawless and you are perceived to be second rate when it comes to service.

Well, Mr. Taylor and Taylor Made Transportation destroys those notions with their first-rate service and professionalism. When you encounter a Taylor Made Transportation employee you will be treated with respect, courtesy, and the utmost professionalism. This is what is demanded from the owner on up. I say from the owner on up because I was taught a long time ago that any great organization is only as strong as its leaders. Those leaders should be the foundation of the organization and then everyone else is built up on them. It's a pyramid but with the owners on the bottom. Mr. Taylor has strong morals and an even stronger work ethic and this is the same expectation that he has of his employees.

Strong morals, good work ethic, and pride in delivering excellent service are three core ingredients for combating the walls of prejudice in any industry. Mr. Taylor and Taylor Made Transportation are equipped with each of them. Although entering the market was not the easiest of things for Mr. Taylor, he has managed to build a name and brand for himself and his company in the transportation industry.

Not wanting to be like the other minorities in the industry Mr. Taylor set out to create a new standard of thinking when it came to doing contracts. Mr. Taylor explains that when he entered the industry most of the minorities that owned businesses were just thinking of subcontracting from larger companies. He did not want to subcontract from anyone and he was going to succeed or fail by doing just that. As you can tell, Mr. Taylor has been successful at what he set out to do. In any industry we as minorities need individuals like Mr. Taylor who are not afraid to step outside the box and step forward and believe that you can do something that others were afraid to do or did not see that they could do.

He is a drum major in his industry because he has shown that when you believe in your vision and you don't allow others to put you in the same category as others. As an entrepreneur you have to be willing to be different if you want to make an impact in your industry. Those who are not willing to take the risk or just want to be ordinary will stay with the pack or fall to the wayside, while those entrepreneurs like Mr. Taylor will separate themselves from the pack and show others how business should be done.

Mr. Taylor says the transportation industry is getting more diverse since he first entered the industry. Mr. Taylor says that the industry was not as professional, computerized or service oriented. Since he has entered into the transportation market it has become more diverse, computerized, and more service oriented. Mr. Taylor prides himself on the service that he is able to provide to his clients.

He says that he has set a standard that those who have been in the industry could only hope to immolate. Understanding customer service and wanting to bring a different style of professionalism to the transportation industry has suited Mr. Taylor just fine. Mr. Taylor defines customer service as "meeting or exceeding the customer's expectations". Yes, we both learned that while in the Hotel / Restaurant Management major at the University of Maryland Eastern Shore. See, you do use that college education later in life.

Mr. Taylor has made sure that his company will stand head and shoulders above the others in his industry by ensuring that he has all of the certifications that are required, being more centralized, and making sure that he dots his I's and crosses his T's. Mr. Taylor says that the transportation industries customer base is expanding due in part to injured soldiers coming home from the war in Iraq, more individuals on dialysis and the increase number of HIV/Aids patients. As America gets older and individuals are living longer they do not drive but still need to get around. There are more disabled individuals today and they still need to get to different places therefore the transportation industry, i.e. Mr. Taylor and Taylor Made Transportation, is the benefactor of the aging and disabling America.

As Mr. Taylor has put it "if the health industry does not get its act together and individuals do not begin to take better care of themselves the transportation industry will be booming for years to come". This is a good thing for Taylor Made Transportation but not so good for individuals. As the industry expands Mr. Taylor wants to see more minorities benefiting from this industry growth. That means that those in the industry must continue to give better customer service, be more professional and gain more of the market share in the industry. Mr. Taylor says, "that there are those who see the growth in the transportation industry and enter it to make a quick buck and then realize that it is not as easy as they thought it would be and then get out of it. This causes the industry to become even more regulated, which is not a bad thing for those who are doing things right but it does have an impact on the industry", says Mr. Taylor.

THE FUTURE

There are other ethnic groups who are also seeing the potential that the transportation industry has going forward. As they see that potential rise they are starting to want to learn more about it and how they can gain from it. There are more Asians who are beginning to look into the transportation industry and are looking to gain a piece of the transportation pie. What will keep Mr. Taylor and Taylor Made Transportation moving into the future and gain an even bigger piece of the transportation pie is being small, diverse, and family oriented.

Being fully certified plays a big part in Taylor Made Transportation being a strong company and aids in gaining the trust of its clients who look to meet with Mr. Taylor personally when they set up meetings with his company. Many people like the personal touch that you get from smaller more personal and family oriented companies. Not every company that is small is personal or family oriented. The larger companies do not necessarily give you the personal touch either because you have to go through other individuals as opposed to dealing directly with the owner of the company.

Being a full service transportation company helps Taylor Made Transportation stand out from its competition because some of them may not offer all of the services that they do. They are also fully bonded which should set well with its clients, because it gives a since of security and stability to the company. Taylor Made Transportation is charging into the future with their fearless commander leading the charge. Mr. Taylor believes that in order to lead one has to be willing to follow. "You have to understand how to take direction too, if you are going to be a good leader. A good leader also knows when to listen and when to speak", Mr. Taylor says.

Mr. Taylor believes when you are a leader or entrepreneur much is expected of you. You have to know that when you are leading those who are behind you are following. As a good leader and entrepreneur you have to be able delegate and understand what you should do and what you should have others doing. I believe great leaders and entrepreneurs surround themselves with good people. They have people around them that buy into their vision and are able to carry it out.

Mr. Taylor has taken the advise that he learned from Mr. Richard Gormley, our Hotel /Restaurant Management Department head, and applied it to his business and would give to other aspiring entrepreneurs, and that is
do it now, make it happen, by any means necessary. He would also tell them to "stick to their dreams, be who you are and do what you do". He also advises any aspiring entrepreneur "to take their time and grow slow". Make sure that it is what you want to do and learn everything that you can about your industry and use it to your advantage. Mr. Taylor has also learned the importance of credit when you are an aspiring entrepreneur.

You must make sure that your personal credit is good but you also will need to be able to put up some collateral. You credit alone will not allow you to go into banks and get a small business loan, Mr. Taylor says. Mr. Taylor initially used "creative financing to start up his business. Using is personal money of $1500 dollars and getting an investor to put up another $1500 dollars, and the initial payment from his first clients, Mr. Taylor has spent the last 10 years making Taylor Made Transportation one of the premier transportation companies in Baltimore, Maryland.

Mr. Taylor says that he eventually went the traditional route of getting more capital for his business but he knew early on that he would have to bring something to the table as well. Mr. Taylor also believes that you must reinvest your money into the company. He says, "Being disciplined and putting the money back into the business is key to you being able to sustain yourself and grow". "You also have to be able to manage your money", Mr. Taylor says. That means, paying your taxes, doing your payroll correctly and keeping accurate records. When you do these things you can't help but have a successful business. Being a young and gifted entrepreneur has not stopped this businessman from wanting to achieve great things.

He believes that being a young entrepreneur has helped him. He believes that he was able to take more risk than he would if he was an older entrepreneur. When you are a young entrepreneur, you are willing to take more risk. Mr. Taylor says, he was single when he started his business so he only had to worry about himself back then. He is now married, and has the family to think about.

From his first contract with Cardinal Gibbons High school to Levindale Geriatric Center, to all the contracts now, Taylor Made Transportation is looking stronger than ever. Going forward Mr. Taylor takes the highs and the lows of his industry in stride. Understanding that his industry has a wealth of potential and he hopes to be able to take advantage of it. He also knows that his industry is not leveraged as all other industries go when it comes to minorities, but with businessmen like Mr. Taylor that is changing for the good.

Mr. Taylor understands that the more minority owned businesses that we have in the different industries we are a part of the more power and control we have in those industries. The transportation industry also does not treat those in the industry fair across the board. The smaller companies do not get the same breaks as the larger companies. This has an effect on the insurance that the smaller companies are able to afford and also the discounts that they get when it comes to insurance.

Being a fan of those who are successful in business Mr. Taylor admires anyone who looks to achieve in business. Mr. Taylor will not have to worry about looking to others who are successful because he has developed his own success story that is not anywhere near finished. Being a diverse company and being able to offer a variety of services to his clients allows him to give his clients better customer services. Being in his industry for 10 years and never missing a payroll bodes well for this transportation juggernaut. Mr. Taylor says that Taylor Made Transportation is his everything next to God and his Wife. He says, "This is how we eat". With his strong morals, high ethics, and great values, this transportation king will be eating well for a very long time!

CHAPTER 13
NURTURING OUR CHILDREN

MONIQUE LEMMON

OWNER
JOYFUL NOISE FAMILY DAYCARE

INTRODUCTION

We are loosing our children. It is becoming a critical condition the way in which we are bringing up our children. It worries me when I look at the world that we live in and the condition of our society as a whole. I do not like to watch the news because it is nothing but negative information being brought into our homes. I happened to be listening to the news and there was a story which entailed a young teen, who had a baby.

The baby had a fever and the young teen, who was the parent, did not know how to break the fever. The story went on to say that the young parent put the child in the refrigerator in order to try to break the baby's fever. At first I did not want to believe what I was hearing and I had to stop for a second and take in what I just heard.

What plagued my mind as I recounted the story was what was going through this young parents mind when they decided to put their child into the refrigerator? I cannot fathom a thought of any parent, in there right mind making the conscience decision to put their child into the refrigerator. There is no part of child rearing that would ever suggest that anyone put a child into a refrigerator. Someone who has never had a child knows that you would never put a child into the refrigerator. In our society today we are faced with so much on our plates and we must deal with work, family issues and just everyday living. We do not need to add to this stress by doing the inconceivable.

We entrust our children to the care of individuals that we believe will take care of them as if it were ourselves watching them. We have to be careful of the individuals that will spend more time with our children then we do on a daily basis. It is imperative that the people we choose to watch over our children have the child's care first and foremost in their minds and hearts. When you watch television you see all the new technology that has been introduced so that we can keep an eye on those that we entrust our children to. From the nanny cam to other technologies that allow us to watch the people who watch our children. Do I think that this technology is an infringement on their rights, yes, do I also believe that our society has changed and we have to be sure that our children are safe, yes. When I think of our children I see what our future can be. We, as parents, are responsible for making sure that our children are taught, cared for and protected. A child's younger years are crucial to what they will become when they get older.

I believe that children are little sponges, take in things and learn core morals, values, and right from wrong between the ages of 3-7. Since we do not spend the majority of our time with our children during these crucial years it is imperative that the individuals that we entrust to spend that time with them teach them all of the vital information that a child needs to learn at those ages and we as parents reinforce that learning.

I am glad that there are people who have chosen to take on the responsibility of nurturing our children when we have to go to work. It does my heart good when I see individuals who have a special love for children that some of us do not have. I believe that it takes a special person to want to care for children. Kids have so much energy and it takes a lot to run after them, keep up with them, and deal with their mood swings.

As adults we think that it is something to deal with co-workers and their mood swings, or our spouses or girlfriends, or boyfriends. This pails in comparison to dealing with children on a daily basis. It can be the most rewarding of times and it can be the most stressing of time. Just ask anyone who has chosen to be a day care provider. They are the unsung heroes of our society just as our teachers are. They are the ones that help to shape and form the minds of our children today. They are our children's second, sometimes first teachers. They usually do not get any publicity unless it is negative.

They usually go unnoticed and unappreciated. What they provide is a service that shapes and forms the minds of our future society. They give tirelessly and provide our children with fun, laughter, and the discipline that is needed more in our society today. In a world going mad it is good to know that there are those out there who see the love in our children's eyes and the warm smiles in their hearts.

The innocence of a child is something that is special. There are those who take that innocence and enjoy nurturing it. There are few who are up to that challenge. I came across one such lady and I am glad to say that she is a member of my church and a fellow Christian. That may not mean much to some people but to those of us in the body of Christ it is good to know that when you leave your child in the care of Ms. Monique Lemmon of **Joyful Noise Daycare,** she is not the only one who is watching over your children. She not only serves the Lord but she is committed to serving the children that she takes care of on a daily basis.

BEGINNINGS

This Baltimore native started out on her trek to entrepreneurship in the catholic school system. Ms. Lemmon spent her younger years in Baltimore city. Being a part of the catholic school system up until high school helped to shape and form this young entrepreneur's foundation for the spiritually strong woman that would become Monique Lemmon.

Attending high school in the Baltimore Public school system would also give her the balance of a private and public school education. It's funny how you talk to people and find out the interesting things that you have in common. I grew up with both a private and public school education and I can see the benefit in both of these forms of education and so did Ms. Lemmon. Ms. Lemmon talked about how the catholic school gave her the spiritual structure that would stay with her through out her growing up and the public school education, which can give you a "real" perspective of how life can be.

When she graduated from Northwestern High School she attended Coppin State University (formerly Coppin State College). She majored in English. Ms. Lemmon believes that her background in education prepped her for becoming an entrepreneur. She says that college gives you the social skills that you will need in being an entrepreneur, as well as math skills that she has to use in order to figure out how many kids she is able to have in her day care. These are things that we thought that we would never use in life but Ms. Lemmon says she found herself using these things to give an example to her stepson.

After beginning college Ms. Lemmon would have to enter the work force and would go to work for a law firm in Baltimore city,and soon found that the corporate world can be cold, callous, and deleterious. The company would close its doors and Ms. Lemmon would find herself seeking employment elsewhere. There are many of us who have experienced the cold hand of the corporate society and have been on the short end of the so called "down sizing" movement. I know that I have traveled that path as well.

Even though Ms. Lemmon experienced the "downsizing" of corporate America she would not allow that to stop her from still achieving and move forward. She began working for the city of Baltimore's Mayor Office of employment. There she would help young people get their GED's, high school diplomas, and find employment. Anyone would feel good about helping individuals achieve the things that I just mentioned but being in this type of position has its downside as well. This particular branch of the city government is funded by grants, as Ms. Lemmon says it was uncertain if the program would receive funding the following year. This can create a nervous condition for anyone who wants to have job stability. There is not a lot of job security in regular corporate America and there is even less security in positions that are predicated on grants.

Knowing that the position did not have a stable future Ms. Lemmon knew that this was not where she belonged. Her desire to own her own business began to get stronger with each day. As the days would go on her vision for being an entrepreneur would way on her heavily. She would decide to look into opening her own daycare and see if that was where God was leading her. Being the Godly woman that she is Ms. Lemmon would trust God and see where he was leading her. Upon getting the information that she would need in order to get her certification for opening a daycare Ms. Lemmon would have to make a decision that would change the rest of her life.

Ms. Lemmon would seek God's advice first and then seek advice from her own supervisor. Her supervisor would give her the nudge that she would need. Monique says, her supervisor told her that even though she would hate to lose her, she believed that God was calling her to better things. That advice would prove to help Ms. Lemmon but not the confirmation that she was looking for.

As Ms. Lemmon put it she would ponder a couple of days about submitting her letter of resignation and would finally give into what God was telling her. She says that she still had not heard from Child Care Administration before she submitted her resignation so there was no guarantee that she was going to be approved. As many of us do we give something to God and we feel that he is not moving fast enough so we want to help him with it.

Ms. Lemmon wanted to do her part in helping God so she would call the Child Care Administration to try and find out about her impending approval but would find no answers. She tells me, "that it was not until I let go of the situation and let God deal with it that I received my answer". That answer would be a yes and Ms. Lemmon would be on her way to the reality that God had envisioned for her. Ms. Lemmon tells me that the ironic thing about opening a daycare was that when her and her husband first got married she did not think that having children was something that she would want to have, as they can be a lot of work, and now she is in the business of taking care of children. You never know what God has in store for you and we never know where he will lead us, we just have to trust him and know that he knows what he is doing. Ms. Lemmon has trusted in the Lord and believed that he knows what he is doing because since that day she has let go and has not looked back and Joyful Noise Daycare has been the result of that faith.

THE INDUSTRY

I remember growing up in northwest Baltimore. It was a small townhouse that was connected to a group of other row houses. We knew most of our neighbors and I played with the kids who also lived in the row homes. It was a small two-bedroom town home and my mother along with my two sisters and I lived there. To this day I still don't know how we all lived in such a small home. Even though it was small it still brings back some great memories of my childhood. My mother was a single parent and raising three children on her own was not easy.

Ever since I can remember my mother has worked two jobs. She did not work two jobs because she wanted to; she worked them because she had to. She was not able to spend a lot of time with us but she made the time that she did spend with us memorable. In our neighborhood there were adults who had all types of jobs and careers. We were not of age to work yet so the task of finding someone to care for us while my mother was at work was made easy for my mother because she was able to find a woman who lived right across the street from us who was what we called back then a babysitter.

Her name was Ms. Watkins. Ms. Watkins was an older woman who had several children of her own, my friends Stuffy, Kirk, and another son and daughter. She also had a husband who we called sport. Ms. Watkins always made things fun and interesting at her house. I remember rushing to her house from school so I could watch captain Chesapeake, Speed Racer, or the Super Friends.

They sure don't make cartoons like they use to uhh. She would fix us lunch that would consist of a hot dog, which was put on toasted bread with butter. I still eat that to this day! We would have some chips and something to drink, and we would either watch our favorite cartoons or go and play outside. Do kids even know what playing outside is anymore? It was a great time that my sisters and I enjoyed as we grew up. Those memories cannot be erased from ones mind because they are forever etched into our lives.

Ms. Watkins would watch us until my mother got home from work and then we would go home for the day. My mom would go to her second job and would make sure that we had something to eat before she left. My older sister would have the responsibility of watching my younger sister and myself until mom got back home. We would get up the next morning and start the same routine all over again. Whenever I ride through the old neighborhood I always look at the corner house that Ms. Watkins still lives in to this day and I get a big ole smile. Thank you Ms. Watkins for taking care of me and my sisters during those adolescent years and for the many lessons that were learned while we were in your care. They are priceless.

There are many people who may look back on their life and have such fond memories as I have had or they may not. In our society today we are running here and there and we drop our children off at the daycare provider without a second thought. The next time that you drop your child or children off at their house or center, just remember that while you are at work memories are being made.

Well, this is a new day and a new time. More and more woman have entered the work force now and there is an even greater demand for daycare providers. One woman who is creating memories with her own daycare is Ms. Lemmon. When she first started researching about home daycare she says that she was disheartened because she found that there were several other home daycare providers in her area already. She did not know if she should even bother to start her own business but after getting further into the research she says she found that it was not as bad as she thought that it was. Ms. Lemmon says that what helped her to feel better about starting this type of business and moving forward was that she began to gain an understanding of her industry. She talked about how she began to understand that when you operate a home daycare service you can only have a certain amount of children. Maryland law says that you can only have one child per certain square inches. She says that when she realized that the daycare providers that were in her neighborhood could only have a certain number of children and that there was such a high demand for daycare providers in her surrounding area, she began to feel a lot stronger about her business and where it could go.

Ms. Lemmon says that the industry is steadily growing and the demand is becoming even greater. She says that daycare providers can only have up to two infants in the home. She says that they require more attention. She says that they are also allowed up to eight toddlers. Ms. Lemmon says that there has been an increase in the number of infants that need to be cared for in this current daycare market. "It is amazing", Ms. Lemmon says "how God has taken me from not being sure if opening a daycare was the right thing to do to having to turn people away because I don't have the space available". She says that within

147

six months of opening her doors she was at the same salary that she had before she had her own business. She attributes Joyful Noise Daycare success to God and holding to the faith in him. Ms. Lemmon believes what separates her Daycare from the others in her industry is that it is not just a daycare.

She says that they also prepare their children for preschool. At Joyful Noise Daycare, you are getting more than a babysitter, Ms. Lemmon says. The parents, her clients also get a curriculum. Their children are exposed to different things through field trips. When her children leave her daycare they are ready for kindergarten. They know colors, shapes, alphabet, and numbers up to their teens. They are able to tell you their name, and phone number.

They are also able to identify parts of their body. With her strong foundation in God and since Ms. Lemmon is a Christian, her business is Christian based and therefore her children get a children's version bible study. What Ms. Lemmon does also is not only keep her children spiritually fit she also keeps them physically fit as well by having them do exercises.

Ms. Lemmon has also developed special activities for the children for each holiday that they celebrate. This young entrepreneur has set the bar very high for those who are in her industry and they could stand to learn a thing or two from this compassionate, but firm leader of the next generation. When it comes to your children and preparing them for the future you know at Joyful Noise Daycare, they are in good hands with Ms. Lemmon.

THE FUTURE

If Joyful Noise Daycare and Ms. Lemmon were a star it would be shining brightly. As the children come and go in and out of the Joyful Noise Daycare experience, they will know that the things that they have learned will help them to be further ahead of the other children that will be entering school with them. Ms. Lemmon looks to make her children's transition from daycare to pre-kindergarten to kindergarten as smooth as possible. As Ms. Lemmon looks forward to moving Joyful Noise Daycare into the future she is positioning it to grow and do even more things in the community.

She hopes that Joyful Noise Daycare will show others that if you have a burning desire to start your own business and you are unsure about it, that you can do it. You must make sure that you do all the research and homework on the industry that you are looking to enter into. She says that you also must talk to others who are in the industry to see how they handle their business. See how and what are the intricacies of that particular industry.

Ms. Lemmon stresses getting to know what it will take to run a business in your particular arena. While Ms. Lemmon says that she did not need to seek financial assistance to begin her business, she says that once Joyful Noise Daycare grows to the point where she is able to move into a center she will look more into capital resources.

She says even though she has not needed to raise capital it has not kept her from looking into ways of gaining financing for the growth of Joyful Noise Daycare. One of the recommendations that she has for young or mature entrepreneurs is a book called the "Red Book". This book is released every few years by the state of Maryland. Very few people are aware of this book she says unless you work for the state.

This book gives a listing of the different industries and the loans and grants that are available for someone looking to get access to capital for a business in certain industries. You can access the red book on line at www.mdredbookonline.com. They may or may not come out with another edition but you can always access the website. The benefit of the Red Book is that the majority of the funds that are listed are for grants. As any entrepreneur will tell you when you can get money that you do not have to pay back you make sure that you do everything within your power to get it.

We as young entrepreneurs do not know about all of the avenues that we can take in order to gain access to start up capital or even capital to grow our business, so it is imperative that the information gets out there so we can take advantage of it. Ms. Lemmon was blessed that she did not have to raise startup capital because the things that she needed in order to start her business were donated to her. She says that she was blessed that a good portion of what she needed for her daycare was given to her.

Ms. Lemmon also says that young entrepreneurs can use other sources that they may have access to capital instead of going the traditional route through banks or other financial institutions. She suggests that you use some of the equity in your home if you own one. You can also use some of your 401k to help you gain the capital that you will need. These are other resources that we may have access to instead of going into debt by getting a loan. We as entrepreneurs must realize as early as possible the importance of having savings and also the value in owning a home.

We have talked about both of these things in previous chapters and I will remind you again of this very crucial lesson that Ms. Lemmon has taught us. I know I wish I knew back then what I know now because it could have groomed me a lot sooner for entrepreneurship. In this modern time with more of us owning homes it is good to know that we have another means to go after our dream of being a young and gifted entrepreneur.

In an industry that you must love in order to be a part of it, Ms. Lemmon says that the children that you have can make you smile even when you do not feel like it. They have an innocence that allows them to help melt all your issues away. Ms. Lemmon says that she loves watching her children try and figure something out and how determined they can get to accomplish something.

She says that it is beautiful to see them take their first steps, say a word, to put a sentence together or to be potty trained and to see the excitement in their faces when they have learned how to go to the bathroom. She says that the only down side to her business is that if everyone is having a bad day and they are just crazy all day. Ms. Lemmon says you got the baby crying, the other kids are cranky for one reason or another and through it all you have to be able to remain calm.

Those moments can be stressful and you have to fight your way through them Ms. Lemmon believes. With the love and support of her husband, whom she loves dearly and admires, it makes those days in the JoyFul Noise Daycare easier to get through. Ms. Lemmon says that she admires her husband because of the love that he has for his family and that he is always there for them and her no matter what. She says that he is not a quitter and helps to push her.

Ms. Lemmon attributes becoming a young and gifted entrepreneur to her mom, Ms. Mary Camper. Growing up in a single family, she learned how to have strength against adversity, and how to lean on faith to get through tough times. She says that her mother's ability to love her children unconditionally, even when they were wrong, gave her an "earthly" insight to how much her heavenly father must love her. She says that her mother always thinks of others and will do without so her family can have the best. Ms. Lemmon says that her mother made growing up without a father seem easy by the way that she balanced work and family. Ms. Lemmon says that her husband is the love of her life but he mother is the center of her heart.

Ms. Lemmon also attributes becoming a young and gifted entrepreneur to her best friend Tina. She says that their lives are so parallel to one another. She says that she admires her strength, her marriage, and her love of her ministry. She is the president of the Genesis nursery ministry at the New Psalmist Baptist Church. Ms. Lemmon says, "that her best friends character is true and what you see is what you get". Ms. Lemmon has surrounded herself with strong individuals and that is vital to anyone being successful in life and being successful as an entrepreneur.

Having her business firmly grounded in Christ and being a doer in this generation of talkers, Ms. Lemmon will be sure to leave a statement of the importance of education. Understanding that anything that you put your mind to and trust God for you can accomplish it, and have her children know that she and her husband trusted God and believed in what they were doing. So as the children go around the house and running up and down the stairs, or they are riding with you in the car asking, "are we there yet" just remember that they all are making a "JoyFul Noise".

CHAPTER 14
PLATINUM STATUS

MAX FORTUNE

PRESIDENT/CEO
THE PLATINUM AGENCY

INTRODUCTION

In certain industries they are different levels for the status that you hold with their company. In the credit card industry, they issue credit cards according to your status level. There are some industries such as network marketing companies that will use different names to describe the various sales levels of their companies. When you have achieved all that you can achieve at certain levels with these companies, you move up to the next level. The government uses numbers to describe the different pay levels of their agencies. You could be a GS-3 or you could be a GS-15. It all depends on how you advance in the particular agency that you work for.

When I did my six-month internship in Atlantic City, New Jersey for the Sands Hotel & Casino, I had the pleasure of learning some valuable lessons. The Sands had what was called a club level in their hotel. The club level was only for special guests who were privy to the benefits of being on this level in the hotel.

They would receive complimentary robes in their suites. They would receive turn down service of their beds, as well as their own lounge where they could watch television. They have complimentary breakfast, and many other privileges that come with being on the club level. These guests were made to feel special because of what they could afford.

American Express is a credit card that is platinum in color. This particular card is platinum in color because it symbolizes exclusive access to privilege. It also represents luxury, customer care that is a cut above the rest. It also represents a level of membership that compliments and enhances its member's lifestyles. Their platinum card provides its members access to a world of privilege and benefits. When you have an American Express Platinum Card, you are made to feel as if you have arrived. When you have an American Express Platinum Card, and are not treated like others who hold other types of credit cards.

What this card gives you is privileges that you would not otherwise have if you did not belong to this credit card club. People will notice you when you pull out an American Express Platinum Card. This world of privilege is not for everyone though. It is only for those who are willing to work for it. You don't get to this level by just wishing for it. You don't get to this level by just asking for it. You have to want it. You have to get up in the morning working for it everyday.

Those who desire it will do whatever it takes to achieve it. They will not stop until they get it. They will be focused, committed, and disciplined and can't rest until they posses it. They live and breathe the privilege. They thirst for it, they crave it, and they pursue it with every fiber of their being. Of course, I am not talking about the American Express Platinum Card, because that won't give you the satisfaction that this will give you. The American Express Platinum Card along with all of the other privileges that I have just mentioned will only give you a certain amount of fulfillment.

The fulfillment that I am talking about is the fulfillment of owning your own business. You can't have that without the desire to go after it. Well, in my quest to bring to those of you who read this book individuals that posses that desire, commitment, and discipline to go after what they want, I found a young and gifted entrepreneur who posses this character. He is bold, determined, gifted, persistent, and magnetic.

He is someone that will leave an impression on you that few others will. He is someone that believes in what he does and will convince you that you should also believe in it. He posses the personality of a lion and the compassion of a dove. What he brings to the table is everything that he has. He is someone that believes in achieving with a capital A. If he were a wine, he would be top shelf.

If he were a plane, he would be first class. His status if it had to be put in a category would definitely be platinum! He is Mr. Max Fortune of **The Platinum Agency**. This is how he rolls when it comes to doing business the Max Fortune way. Don't let the name fool you. I thought the same thing when I first heard his name, it can't be real. But it is, and he is one of our young and gifted entrepreneurs.

BEGINNINGS

This spirited young entrepreneur was born in New Haven, Connecticut and moved to Maryland when he was 3 years old. He attended Loyola High School located in Towson, Maryland. He entered Morgan State University, attended for 2 years, and then left school to pursue other opportunities. Mr. Fortune would take his strong desire to run his own business and his quick learning ability and put them to the test. Believing in his ability to be successful Mr. Fortune began working different sales jobs that would hone his skills as a salesman.

He sold insurance policies, vacuum cleaners, furniture, and cars. Each of these jobs would take him to new levels of understanding of what the real business world was like. Mr. Fortune was determined at a very young age. He married at a young age and would be counted on by his family as the sole bread winner in the household. Having that kind of pressure as a young black man could have caused the average man to succumb to the pressure but Mr. Fortune was not the average man and certainly was not an individual to see the negative in his situation.

He took the challenge and worked hard at what he did and turned each problem into a positive opportunity. Mr. Fortune is an individual who does not take the pressure to perform lightly. He is someone who has stepped up to the challenge when he was called upon to perform. His desire to be the best at what he does is only matched by his pursuit of success.

Mr. Fortune believes that he got his entrepreneurial spirit from watching his mother who was also an entrepreneur. He says that watching her had a very positive impact on him and wanting to run his own business. Mr. Fortune says that he had his first taste of entrepreneurship when he and his friend started their own hot dog stand during the summer of his freshman and sophomore years at Morgan State University.

Mr. Fortune has had several business ventures since his first one during that summer. He has sold fire extinguishers door to door, a snowball stand, he has owned a record label, and a magazine, as well as run an entertainment business. So as you can see Mr. Fortune has a thirst for achievement and is not afraid to take on the challenge of starting a business.

Many individuals are afraid to take the step into entrepreneurship. Mr. Fortune is not one of those individuals. Mr. Fortune likens getting his first taste of entrepreneurship to athletics. He says "it's like in golf when you get a whole in one, or you hit your fist home run. You get such a rush and a great feeling that you spend the rest of your time chasing that feeling ". "You want to gain that achievement over again and you don't stop until you can do it again".

Mr. Fortune has used each business venture to build on and to help shape him into the businessman that he is today. Building a business from the ground up is not for the weak at heart. There will come rejections and disappointments that will cause you to question whether or not you made the right decision.

Mr. Fortune has taken the disappointments of being laid off from jobs and used it to create his own destiny. He says that when he was working on one job and was passed over for a more prominent role with this particular company he knew that it was time for him to branch out and pursue his vision of entrepreneurship and take it to the next level. That next level would be Platinum Agency. Mr. Fortune would not go the traditional route of starting a business by going to a financial institution to obtain a small business loan. He took money from his last paycheck which was around $500+ dollars along with another $525 dollars that he borrowed from his wife. He spent the first several months working his business out of his home and used that $1000 dollars to purchase some office space, purchase a desk, a phone, a chair, and pay for the first months rent. He would start with such humble means and would build Platinum Agency into a strong flourishing agency.

Mr. Fortune tells me that his goal is to be a millionaire by the time he turns 35 and to be a billionaire, yes I said billionaire, by the time he is 45. He is the first person that I have met that said this to me. Not just for this project but ever! This shows me that Mr. Fortune is focused and determined in what he wants to achieve. I myself had not put such aggressive goals on myself. I of course wanted to own my own business but I never thought in terms of the type of goals that Mr. Fortune did. That is the issue that many of us as black men and women have.

We do not see ourselves going beyond the reachable. Mr. Fortune has gone beyond the thinkable and made the unthinkable achievable. It is achievable because Mr. Fortune believes that it is achievable. When you believe in something, you must pursue it with reckless abandonment. It must become your driving force as it has become for Mr. Fortune. "We have to stop thinking of ourselves as second class citizens", says Mr. Fortune. We have to believe that we can achieve and be successful entrepreneurs. What we have to believe in is each other. The stronger we feel about each other the more we will support each other. What has disappointed me the most is the lack of effort that we have in supporting our own businesses. Many other ethnic groups support their own businesses but when it comes to our community we lag far behind.

The more we have individuals like Mr. Fortune, who are making a concerted effort to change the mindset of our communities, the more we will begin to see ourselves in a different light. Mr. Fortune and the Platinum agency help individuals with their taxes as well as their credit situations. Many of us are going into debt and are unsure how to even begin to get out of it.

While our incomes are remaining stagnant, the cost of living is increasing steadily. What Mr. Fortune is doing with Platinum Agency is helping individuals realize how to create healthy credit. Healthy credit is crucial to anything that you want to do in your life. If you want to start your own business, you have to make sure that your credit is alive and thriving. So many people today have credit that is in critical condition.

We are flat lining our potential when we do not take care of our credit and our taxes. Your taxes are crucial to you running your own business. None of us can afford to have our taxes out of order, especially those of us who own a business or hope to own one. Mr. Fortune and the Platinum Agency staff are in business to make sure that your personal taxes and your credit are in order and will give you the opportunity to be able to do the things that you want to do.

When you deal with the Platinum Agency, you deal with an agency that treats each customer not like gold, bronze or silver but like its name Platinum. Its customers will encounter service that is first class and second to no one else in its industry. To Mr. Fortune and the Platinum Agency family every customer is special.

THE INDUSTRY

It's the time of year that every employee, who is anticipating a refund check from the government looks forward to receiving their W-2 forms. It's tax time! The time of year when those who look to be ahead of the game and receive their refund back before you can say IRS. When you look to get your taxes done you need to be sure that the firm that you decide or the individual that you decide to do your taxes is trustworthy. Not having your taxes done properly can mean a heap of trouble for a business or an individual. Just ask Enron, WorldCom, or Wesley Snipes. You have to be sure that your taxes are in order. You must make sure that you have accurate records and that you have someone who will use your accurate records to get you all the money back that you deserve.

When it comes to taxes, it's all about record keeping and making sure that you do not owe any money. Some people can deal with not getting a refund just as long as they do not owe. Not owing is the major thing that we want to avoid.

If we can walk away each year and not have to give the government back any money, we are happy. How any of us wind up owing money is beyond me. We have to make sure that we have enough money taken out during the course of the year so that we do not have to give anything back when it is tax time.

If you choose to hire someone such as Mr. Fortune and The Platinum Agency, you must be sure that they have your best interest at heart. They must have character, integrity, and have a strong knowledge of the industry. These are characteristics that Mr. Fortune and his staff operate with. It should be a comfort to you when you take your taxes to someone who knows the ins and outs of the tax laws and is able to get you money back that you might not have been able to had they not been doing your taxes. The more we get back in taxes the happier we are and Mr. Fortune and the Platinum Agency family wants his clients to be happy.

The credit repair industry is growing by leaps and bounds. It is growing because our society is driving themselves deeper and deeper into debt. Many people spend money that they do not have and spend the next year wallowing in the debt that they have created for themselves. They will run up their credit cards buying gifts for people that they do not even like, or do not like them. They will spend money that could have been better used or even invested.

I was reading a book recently entitled "Nickel and Dime Your Way to Wealth", by Ms. Deborah Owens. In this book, she discusses the importance of people getting out of debt, and using their money to create wealth. She talked about the way that we spend our money on gifts at Christmas time. Her suggestion was that we buy gifts that will help individuals grow financially. She mentioned that instead of buying a gift that would only last for a short period of time, that we buy gifts that will last and possibly gain value. She suggested buying someone 1 share of stock from a company where they use their products. She also suggested that we give our children things that will maintain their value or increase in value, such as trust funds, or mutual funds. I would also say that we must begin to realize the importance of real estate.

It is one of the very few things that will appreciate in value. If we are going to get out of this being in debt mentality then we have to begin to change our way of thinking. Mr. Fortune and the Platinum Agency are geared to help individuals start changing their minds. When you change a person's way of thinking you change their way of living. Individuals like Mr. Fortune are needed more and more because people's spending habits have become poorer and poorer. With the cost of living increasing and our incomes remaining stagnant or decreasing, it is becoming very important that we start to spend our money in a much better way.

Mr. Fortune believes that his industry is changing as people's economic situations change. He says, the internet is changing the way that people use attorneys these days. He says that people are seeking attorneys less and less because the internet has given them access to more information and has made it easier for individuals to do things for themselves. "They will only seek attorney's for those things that you really need to hire them for", says Mr. Fortune. The information super highway is helping people to become more empowered, I believe.

They are gaining access to more information which means they are adopting the do it yourself mentality. The more things that we are able to do ourselves the less we will have to depend on others or pay others to do it for us. This ultimately will have a great impact on the money that we have to spend. We will not have to spend as much money on paying someone else for something that we can do.

This in turn puts more money in our pockets, which we can then use to pay off some of our debt. The credit repair industry is an emerging industry because of where our country is heading. We are becoming a society of haves and have-nots. Those who have are securing their futures so they do not have to worry about the future. Those who have not are becoming more in debt trying to maintain a reasonable way of living.

Mr. Fortune likens being in this industry or any other industry for that matter, like being a boxer. Mr. Fortune says that a boxer gets hit constantly but does not go down. The only punch that knocks a boxer down is the one that he does not see, says Mr. Fortune. He says that the punch that a boxer does not see knocks him down because he is not prepared for the impact of the punch. When you are prepared for the impact you can brace for it, says Mr. Fortune.

Many of us have to prepare ourselves for the impact, whether in business or in life, says Mr. Fortune. The more prepared we are the less of a chance we will be knocked down. In any industry or in life we will get knocked down and the question is will you get up? If it is up to Mr. Fortune and the Platinum Agency, they will see to it that many of us who have been knocked down not only get back up, but get back up and get even stronger.

THE FUTURE

"When it's all said and done I want to be known as someone who helped change the minds of a generation of people, and the way we think about our financial situation". These are the words of Mr. Fortune and what he looks to accomplish and leave behind. In our lives we meet people and they are in our lives for a reason (long-term) or a season (short-term). They can have a positive impact on your life or they can have a negative impact on your life.

Mr. Fortune and the Platinum Agency wants to be one of those people and companies that have a positive impact in your life. When you walk into the office of the Platinum Agency you will be made to feel as if someone cares about your future. Mr. Fortune does not believe in just working on one thing at a time and that is why he says that he is planning on doing things in the future that will overhaul the mindset that we have of thinking like second-class citizens.

One thing that any entrepreneur understands is diversity. When I say diversity I mean in respect to the services that a business offers as well as the number of industries that exist. Mr. Fortune is one of those entrepreneurs who understands the value that his agency has in being able to offer various services to his clients. In this day and time being able to go to one company for a number of services is key to being around in the future. The more diverse that you are the more longevity you create for yourself. Mr. Fortune has also created longevity for himself because of the multiple streams of income that he has created for himself.

When you don't have all of your eggs in one basket so to speak you are able to balance the cash flow that you will have for yourself and your business, and Mr. Fortune has done that for himself and for the Platinum Agency. As an entrepreneur you must always be thinking progressively. I love to be around individuals who don't just think for the moment. Individuals who can see past the moment and always want to keep it moving are the ones that keep ahead of the bell curve.

Mr. Fortune and the Platinum Agency are all about is being ahead of the bell curve. They are what I call extraordinary. They don't act like others, they don't think like others, they don't work like others, and they don't believe like others. That is what separates the average person from the go-getter, and the successful people. What we have to understand is that to be successful now and in the future you have to believe and see yourself as a part of that future. You can only go as far as you are willing to take yourself. Mr. Fortune wants to see people and other entrepreneurs go further than you think that you can go. In order to do that we have to change the way we think. Think positive, think progressive, think big, think Platinum!

ERNEST BURLEY JR.

OWNER
BURLEY INSURANCE AND FINANCIAL SERVICES

INTRODUCTION

Ernest Burley has been with State Farm Insurance Companies for over 17 years. He started in the operations side of the company in the claims area. He was born in New Rochelle, New York, but was raised in Miami, Florida since the age of 5. He moved to Maryland in 1996 to open a State Farm agency. On January 1, 1997, Ernest opened his doors as a State Farm agent.

Ernest is a born again Christian, who attends First Baptist Church of Glenarden, where Pastor John K. Jenkins Sr. presides. He is an usher who loves what he does-ushering people into the house of the Lord and helping them however he can.

In addition to being a State Farm agent, Ernest is also a Certified Financial Planner™. His office is Burley Insurance and Financial Services, Inc. Ernest loves equipping people with insurance and financial services. His desire is to equip people with the knowledge (and products) needed to live a fruitful and fulfilling life. Ernest is licensed in MD and DC for all insurance and investment products but also holds licenses in Florida, Georgia, NY, and VA for investment products.

Ernest loves to help clients meet their needs through Asset Protection, Wealth Accumulation, and Financial Management.
Are you prepared for your future? Do you know how you will be able to afford to live during retirement? If you were to pass away today what assets would you have to leave to your children or your children' s children. The bible says in **Proverbs 13:22 - A good man leaveth an inheritance to his children's children, and the wealth of the sinner is laid up for the just. (KJV).**

One of the most important things that I hope that each and everyone that is reading this book gets out of it is the importance of preparing for the future. Social security is going to be virtually non-existent when those of us in the 25-45 age range get to retirement age. We must now begin to look at our money management, our health, and our legacies. We have to begin now to understand what we are doing with our money. This generation of individuals has to become more diligent in preparing not only ourselves for the future but those who will be coming behind us.

Those of us in the Black community have been mistaken into thinking that our wealth is in what we wear or what we drive. Nothing could be further from the truth. There is nothing that we wear or drive that increases in value. Value is added to things that we live in, invest in, or businesses that we own. Once we begin to understand what that means then we can move forward and pass on the inheritance that the aforementioned bible verse discusses.

We will also begin to pass on knowledge to not only our children but our children's children. This is the foundation of building wealth. We not only have to build wealth but we must also protect what we are building. Any smart businessman or woman knows that when you work hard for something and put all of your blood, sweat, and tears into it you want to make sure that you keep it and are able to pass it on to those who will come behind you. As an entrepreneur you want to make sure that is around for years to come. That cannot happen if you do not take the time to ensure its protection.

There are individuals that will show you how to take care of your assets and then there are those who want to make sure that you understand where the best opportunities are for your money and investments. I was introduced to a gentlemen that believes in people not only looking at the here and now but looking down the road into their future. He wants to see people begin to have their money working for them instead of them working for their money. There are some people who work hard and then there are some that work smart. When you meet this young entrepreneur you know that he is about working smart. Meet Mr. Ernest Burley of **Burley Insurance and Financial**

Services, Inc. He is taking individuals from working for their money to their money working for them.

BEGINNINGS

This Florida native got his start as a young man growing up in the Miami area. He attended the University of Florida and graduated with a degree in Economics. After graduating he found himself wanting to enter corporate America but as most of us find out the jobs that were available were not paying enough. Mr. Burley would wind up going to work for the State Farm Company, he would begin with State Farm in the operations division, where he focused on the claims side of the division dealing with home owners claims. After spending 3 years in the operations division he was promoted and proved to be a great asset to the State Farm Company. He was responsible for reinspecting claims of the other employees and to train new employees on the State Farm way of doing things.

Mr. Burley built a career with State Farm, worked for them and created opportunities for himself that would pay off for him in the years to come. Many of us have used our early experiences and knowledge to help build our careers and businesses. What a lot of us have done in the past is buy into the misconception that we have to spend the rest of our lives working for some instead of working for ourselves. What Mr. Burley has done is to combine the two together. He grew with the company and then used that company to launch his own business. We have talked about franchises in a previous chapter but in this chapter we will take a look at it from a different perspective with Mr. Burley and the Burley Insurance and Financial Services Inc. as our guide.

Mr. Burley used his years of experience with State Farm to start his business in insurance and financial services. It would not be easy though. State Farm as any other franchisee has strict criteria that you must meet in order to own your own franchise. Mr. Burley would seek this opportunity when it presented itself to him. Any of us would be hesitant because of the uncertainty of starting your own business. Mr. Burley was no exception but he would push through his apprehension and would trust God and go forward.

After qualifying for his own franchise with State Farm Mr. Burley opened his office doors at the beginning of 1997. Mr.

165

Burley talked to me about the difference between having a franchise as opposed to owning your business. He says, "With his particular company State Farm will provide financing for the first year so that you can meet your business obligations and then you are on your own". He says, "that it is good to have the backing of a fortune 500 company behind you but it is not easy".

THE INDUSTRY

Too many of us in this day and time only think about the here and now. We do not think about our future. If there is one thing that I want everyone to get out of reading this book is that we must prepare for our future. When I look at our society and see the conditions in which the majority of us live in it upsets me. It upsets me because I know that we can do and be so much more. One of the major purposes of this text is to show that we can be and do so much more. I had a conversation with my best friend the other day and we were talking about where the black community spends its money. As I write this particular chapter it is just past the Christmas holiday and this year is quickly coming to an end and a new one will be beginning in a few days.

My best friend and I stated the fact that black people are the largest consumers in this country and I believe the Latino community would follow closely behind in second. He stated that even though we are the largest consumers we make the lowest average salaries. I posed this question to him. "What does that say about us, and what does it say about what we spend our money on?" His answer as well mine is that we spend our money on things and not on investing. Many of us do not buy things that increase in value but rather decrease in value.

We need to begin to think in terms of long-term instead of short-term. We need to move towards having our money working for us instead of us working for our money. Many of us are in the cycle of comfort and are not looking to our futures. Our spending habits say a lot about us as individuals and as business owners. Getting our communities to see the importance of where our money is being spent and used should be on the top of all of our priorities, I know that it is on mine. Another person that I know believes in putting our money in places that will secure our future is Mr. Burley.

Mr. Burley not only insures people but he is also a Certified Financial Planner, so he helps individuals get their money to work for them. In the insurance and financial planning industry you must get people to see the value in investing their money. Having the correct type of insurance is an investment. You need someone who will put your well being first when it comes to coverage.

Having the wrong type of coverage can be devastating to someone. Just ask the residents of New Orleans, Mississippi, and Alabama, now that the clean up has begun after Hurricane Katrina. It is absurd to me that in this day and time that individuals would have to battle for something that is rightfully theirs. The insurance industry is taking a hit because some insurance companies are not honorable. They are more concerned about their bottom line then the welfare of their customers. There are many scandals out here that would make any insurance company skeptical of the many claims that are filed on a daily basis, but there are even more claims that are legitimate and should be paid.

It is good to know that there are owners such as Mr. Burley, who believes in treating his customers with respect and professionalism. He believes that when a customer walks into your business they should be acknowledged immediately. "Your clients must be shown that you are concerned about them", says Mr. Burley. You must always take your clients into consideration", says Mr. Burley.

There is a distinct difference between those who are considerate of their customers and those who are not, and as respectable a man as Mr. Burley is you know that as one of his clients you will be treated with compassion and respect. When Mr. Burley first started in his industry and with the State Farm Company he says that it was mainly a provider of Auto, Life, and Fire Insurance. As his career grew with State Farm, State Farm also expanded as a company and began to delve into the financial service market. Mr. Burley says that his company is gearing more towards the financial management and asset management industry now and will continue in that market segment in the future.

Financial management is a key component to all of our futures. Knowing where to invest our money and what to invest our money in is what will keep us from having to worry about our futures and know that they are secure. Many of our parents did not talk to us about preparing for our futures. Our parents are approaching or have approached retirement age and they will be or are collecting their Social Security pensions or if they were wise they also had other investments such as an IRA, stocks, bonds, or mutual funds. For some people these things are new.

Especially when it comes to our generation. We think that we are young and invincible but the truth be told, time waits for no one. Just as our parents got older so will we. If we do not do things now that will give us a future all will be lost. Mr. Burley and his firm are here to make sure that we do have a future and he is someone that will help you understand how to properly prepare for it.

Many in the financial management industry will leave you disheartened because they will make you feel as if all they want is your money and then will disappear. This is far from the truth when it comes to Mr. Burley and Burley Insurance and Financial Services. His genuine concern for his people, his clients, and those he deals with is what separates him from others in his industry. He has a sound spiritual foundation, which is why he has the respect of not only his clients but those who come to work for him.

He believes in going beyond what may be asked of him and his business. Mr. Burley talked with me about how he had a client that was completing a payment for his services and they only accept money orders or checks. His client was an older person and would have to walk up the street to a nearby 7-11 in order to complete this transaction. So Mr. Burley took it upon himself to drive the lady to the store so that she could get the money order and then drove back to the office so that they could complete the transaction.

Now, Mr. Burley says that most people in business yet alone in his industry would not have done what he did but that is what separates him from others". As you can see Mr. Burley is not only willing to meet the needs of his clients but he is willing to exceed them as well. In this day and time that will take you a long way not only in the financial service industry but in any service industry. Mr. Burley also believes that having a firm

168

belief in God separates him from others. Mr. Burley is a strong believer in following up on your contacts. He says, "that you should collect everyone's information and then follow up with them". This is something that I am a strong advocate of. There are too many businessmen and women who do not take the time to follow up on any type of level. Whether it is a potential client or returning a phone call or email from someone trying to get in contact with them.

I believe that when you do not follow up with people no matter what it is it is very unprofessional. The person took the time to contact you and you should show them the courtesy of getting back to them. I think that people only get back to those individuals that they want to get back in contact with, which is a sad statement to make. I cannot tell you how many people say to me when I return their phone call, "I tried to get in contact with this person and they never got back to me". Getting back to someone could mean the difference between you getting a client and loosing a client, and no entrepreneur wants to see money get away.

With his tenacious and persistence this young entrepreneur is poised and prepared to give the financial management industry the respect and progressive outlook that is needed in this day and time. The financial management industry could use a few more business people like Mr. Burley because when you are talking about asking people to trust you with their money you must first show yourself trustworthy. Mr. Burley is proving to be one of the trustworthy people not just in his industry but in any industry today. This will no doubt keep him and his company around for years to come and will take them into the future.

THE FUTURE

Financial management is something that we as minorities need more of. I cannot stress enough the importance of understanding your money but also where you put your money. People's financial situations are moving in the wrong direction and the only way that we can begin to change it is by educating ourselves. The more we read the more we begin to understand and the more we learn. If we are to begin to bring ourselves from the current mindset that we are in when it comes to our economic situations we have to change our way of thinking. We have to think more progressively and be more focused and disciplined in our spending. When we can think in terms of years instead of the here and now then we can begin to progress as individuals, businessmen and women, and as entrepreneurs. We can't depend on anyone but ourselves. If we do not do it then who will? The overall economy of this country and the larger global economy is changing, and if we do not move with that change we will get left behind.

Mr. Burley and the Burley Insurance and Financial Services Inc. is here to see that we stay a part of the global economy. We can ensure our futures by sacrificing and saving. "We have to be sure that we save money and put it where we can get the most use out of it", says Mr. Burley. That is what you will get when you walk into Burley Insurance and Financial Service Inc., you get a firm that is focused on helping you save money and put it where you will get the most use out of it. When you deal with Mr. Burley and his staff you will come out feeling that you are not working harder for your money but you are working smarter with your money.

Since the financial security level of individuals is so unstable in our present day society the financial management industry is looking stronger by the day. The industry is impacting people's lives in one-way or another. As Mr. Burley says, " there are not many individuals that are not touched by the insurance and financial management industry.

Impacting individuals' lives one client at a time is what Mr. Burley and his firm does. Positively impacting his community is what Mr. Burley seeks to do and it brings him great pleasure when he knows that his clients' assets are adequately protected. He also prides himself in helping his clients build wealth. Mr. Burley believes that we should all leave a legacy behind. What he longs to be remembered for is that he loves the Lord, and that he left something behind to carry on. He says, "Many of us do not have anything that we leave behind".

Mr. Burley believes that has to change. With Burley Insurance and Financial Services Inc. you get a company that will help you leave something behind. They have a plethora of services and products that will meet your need and that is the key to any company surviving. So whether you are in need of insurance protection or you are in need of financial management and planning, you can rest assured that Mr. Burley will see to it that your policy is done right and that your finances are protected because God's got his back and he in turn has your back!

FINANCIALMANAGEMENT
VOCABULARY

IRA - Individual Retirement Annuity that qualifies for certain tax advantages.

Mutual Fund - An investment company which ordinarily stands ready to buy back its shares at their current net asset value; the value of the shares depends on the market value of the fund's portfolio securities at the time. Mutual Funds generally continuously offer new shares to the investor.

Money Market Deposit Account (MMDA) - A market-sensitive bank account available since December 1982. Such accounts are required to have a minimum of $1,000 (until January 1, 1986), and only three checks can be drawn per month. Interest rates are comparable to rates on money market funds, though any particular bank's rate can be higher or lower.

Annuity (ANN) -
   (1)   A scheduled payment to a retired person.
   (2)   A series of equal payments at fixed intervals.

Bond - An interest-bearing certificate of debt, usually issued in series, by which the issuer obligates itself to pay the principal amount at a specified time, usually five years or more after date of issue, and to pay interest periodically usually semiannually.

Certificate of Deposit (CD) - A negotiable, nonnegotiable or transferable receipt payable to the depositor for funds deposited with a bank, usually interest bearing.

Stock - The legal capital of a corporation divided into shares.

Price-Earnings Ratio (P/E) - The price of a share of stock divided by earnings per share for a 12-month period.

CHAPTER 16
THE ART OF REAL ESTATE INVESTING

SANDRA PEARSALL

REAL ESTATE INVESTOR

INTRODUCTION

Ms. Pearsall was born and raised in Baltimore, Maryland. She attended public school but she did not graduate from high school. She was able to obtain her GED later; she got off to a late start living on her own by the age of 17. Many times working 2 jobs at a time to make ends meet. She started investing in real estate in 2002 at the age of 31, starting from zero. By the time she turned 34 she had already reached financial freedom. She was able to quit my job. She now has 14 properties from Maryland to North Carolina and over 1.5 million in real estate. She recently published her first book entitled "Let Real Estate Work For You As It's Doing For Me". Her book is a straight-forward guide on her life and real estate investing. Designed for beginners to obtain the knowledge to be successful in the real estate business.

In 2006 she was named the National Real Estate Investor of the Year. Financial freedom is reachable with the right knowledge and motivation. The best advice she can give is to associate yourself with positive people who you can learn from such as your local Real Estate Investors clubs. Don't think about investing anymore, just do it! You'll be glad you did.

When I started this project my goal was to show young entrepreneurs that were in different industries and were looking to enlighten, empower, and invest in other individuals. I also wanted to show the importance of us being represented in an array of industries.

There are industries that we covered so far in the book that I believe play a relevant role in us as a people gaining the economic leverage that we need. There are industries that we covered in this book that gave us insight into making our lives better both internally and externally. We have also looked at industries that play a role in our everyday lives.

One of the most important things that I wanted to achieve when I decided to embark on this project was to change the mindset of our communities as a whole. I wanted to help take us from a working for someone mentality to an owning our own business mindset. You cannot change someone's direction until you first change their way of thinking. Many of us are on jobs that we do not like and are unhappy with our work environments.

The people that we spend more time with than our families are individuals that push us to the very edge of our tempers. We endure these jobs because we feel secure in having that paycheck deposited into our bank account on a weekly, bi-weekly, or monthly basis. What we fail to realize is that as soon as the check hits the account or even before the check hits the bank account the money is gone.

We will not decide to change the way we think until we begin to get sick and tired of working paycheck to pay check hoping that the job that we hold on to does not decide to let us go. The truth be told there is not a job out here today that is secure. Even entrepreneurship is no guarantee. The only thing that we can do is to make sure that we make the best decisions that we can and trust God in those decisions.

One industry that I believe is one of the best industries that we can be a part of is the real estate industry. We discussed the real estate industry in prior chapters but in this chapter we will look at it from an investment standpoint. When I was thinking of the different industries that I wanted to cover in this book I knew that I wanted to cover the real estate industry from an investment perspective because it is one of the major ways that we can gain access to wealth. I do not know when we will realize that real estate is one of the only things that we buy that appreciates and can be an asset to you.

Buying a house or land is one of the most sound investments that any of us can make. We can keep it and leave it for our children or our children's children, or we can sell it and use the money that we will make from the deal, hopefully, to invest in something else or do even greater things with it. While doing this project I was introduced to a woman who had an amazing story and an extraordinary personality.

She is someone that decided to take on the challenge of the real estate industry and is proving that we can build wealth through real estate investing. Meet Ms. Sandra Pearsall, Real Estate Investor, someone who is taking the real estate industry one investment at a time!

BEGINNINGS

This Baltimore native did not grow up on easy street. As many of us know who are from Baltimore, or any other urban city, life ain't been no crystal stair. Ms. Pearsall was not from a middle class home nor was she born with a silver spoon in her mouth. As she put it " being broke is what I learned as a young child. Mama was always broke. We went without a lot. Many times Mama did not have any money to feed us. Most of the people in my neighborhood had nothing but we always managed to have even less than them."

Ms Pearsall dropped out of high school at the age of 16 and was living on her own by the age of 17, but even earlier then that at the age of 9 her parents had split up. By the age of 19 she was married, and then divorced six years later. After receiving her GED, Ms. Pearsall would find herself working on jobs, some barely making minimum wage. She would work two jobs to make ends meet. Ms. Pearsall has always had a strong determination and motivation.

She saved up enough money to take the nursing assistant training, which would quickly land her a job making $5.25 per hour. This was about $2.00 more per hour then she was making at the restaurants that she had previously worked for. She would then work for a nursing home for 4 years. Being the strong motivated individual that Ms. Pearsall is she received several promotions on her job, but was still not making a comparable salary. As she says, " I was still getting nowhere fast."

Believing that there was more for her then she was currently getting Ms. Pearsall sought to make a change in her life. Many of us talk about making our lives better but there are those few, such as Ms. Pearsall, who actually make their lives better. She is one of those in our generation who has moved from being a part of this talking generation to the doing generation. One only has to look at where Ms. Pearsall started from and see where she is now to understand what needs to be done to move all of us from a talking generation to a doing generation.

Self-motivation is one of the key ingredients to our generation moving forward into the economic leverage stage that we are moving towards. Believing in oneself is also a key ingredient to achieving economic leverage and financial freedom.

Ms. Pearsall knew that if she stayed on the current path that she had taken then she would continue to reap the same results. By 2002 Ms. Pearsall decided that she had had enough of that lifestyle. She could not allow herself to continue to live paycheck to paycheck and working 2 jobs just to make ends meet. Simply put Ms. Pearsall got sick and tired of being sick and tired. She decided to do something about her situation. The decision that she would make would be the beginning of something special.

None of us knows what our future will bring. Some of us will enjoy sitting in our day to day lives and feel secure in the jobs that we hold. We are content living pay check to pay check believing that what we are doing is what we will continue to do for the remainder of our lives.

Many of us today have become comfortable with this lifestyle. We do not want to take any risk nor do we want to do anything that will jeopardize our receiving that paycheck at the end of the week. There are some of us who make a six figure income and some of us who are in the lower income levels, but the mentality is the same. We do not want to do anything about our current situation or help others to improve theirs. Ms. Pearsall was not one of those people. She was someone who was on the lower end of the economic totem pole, but her mentality was that of a millionaire. She did not allow her environment to dictate who she was or where she would end up.

We encounter individuals that say that they want better for themselves but very rarely do people follow through with making life better for themselves. Ms. Pearsall not only talked about it she did something about it. She even began her own cleaning service business to help her journey into entrepreneurship.

As any business owner knows you must have good workers in order to keep a business growing. That would be the Achilles heal of Ms. Pearsall's first business venture. She would use that experience to launch herself into her quest to conquer the world of real estate. Believing in her destiny to become financially free Ms. Pearsall set out to become a real estate investor. She says that when she first started out she had individuals that were telling her that she was taking a big risk, and what if things did not work out. Ms. Pearsall used that negativity and turned it into positive motivation. She said her response to those who said that she was taking a big risk was " I would rather risk making money then risk being broke."

Ms. Pearsall says that most of the negative comments about becoming a real estate investor was made by people who knew absolutely nothing about real estate or who did not own anything. She did not let those people influence what she felt in her heart. She was willing to take the risk to be financially free instead of sitting and doing nothing. She would take the equity that she had in her primary home and would make her first investment.

She would net $400 in positive cash flow from that deal. She tells the story of her first purchase in her book "Let Real Estate Work For You As It's Doing For Me", published in 2005. She said that a few days before she was to go to closing for the property she sat outside the house contemplating whether or not it was the right thing to do. She says that she did not have anyone who had taught her about real estate, nor did she know what she was really doing.

She was thinking of pulling out of the deal and she says that she started to pray. She says that she turned on the radio and the song "What God has for me is for me", was playing and she knew then that it was right for her. She closed on that property. She paid $80,000 for the property and it is now worth $280,000. She says, I am glad that I decided to go ahead with that deal. It changed my life"!

THE INDUSTRY
Who's Afraid To Be A Millionaire? That is the title of the book that I am currently reading. This book puts the challenge to the everyday lay person to grab hold of their fear of their finances

177

and to begin to build wealth so that they can begin to secure their futures. One of the wealth building strategies that this book talks about is home ownership.

The real estate industry is coming out of one of its most productive gains that it has ever seen. The 1990's proved to be one of the most lucrative decades for home ownership, as well as real estate investment. As I mentioned earlier real estate is one of the only investments that does not depreciate. Here in the 21st century the real estate market has gone into a decline. Over the past several years the real estate industry has had an increase in the number of houses that are for sale and less people looking to purchase them.

Any good business owner knows that when you have more supply then you have demand the prices of your product or service will go down. It goes down because you have too much inventory in your possession and you do not make money off of inventory that sits idle. This fact is true for the housing market today. There is a surplus of homes on the market, which is causing home owners and potential sellers, to come down on their asking prices for their properties.

The surplus market has also forced real estate sellers to offer other incentives to potential buyers to make the deals more attractive. Sellers are also offering to pay the closing cost for buyers. Houses have reached new levels of what they cost, which has prevented individuals from being able to afford many of the houses on the market.

Salaries are not increasing with the cost of living and therefore it is causing the government to create programs that will make homes more affordable. Although there has been an increase in the number of minority homeownership the number of foreclosed homes is increasing as well as tax sale properties. The newspapers are filled with news about the real estate market on a daily basis. Banks have to lower interest rates so that people will be able to afford the monthly mortgage on a home.

The prices of homes is getting out of control. While the prices have gone up the amount of square footage is going down. There are many areas in the Baltimore vicinity that I believe are very overpriced. The real estate market will not prove to be beneficial for some but for others it can be quite lucrative. There are some who are getting the lemonade out of what others see as a lemon of a real estate market. Just ask Ms. Pearsall. Since 2002 she has acquired 14 properties and has been able to propel herself into the elite of the real estate investor market.

When Ms. Pearsall started in real estate investing the market was just entering into its down turn. We had just had the devastation of 9/11 and the country was entering into the war on Iraq. All the signs were saying stop! However, Ms. Pearsall saw the green light, began to grab hold of the real estate industry, and has not let go since. The real estate industry is now entering into a significant down slide and for the moment is not showing signs of recovering anytime soon. This loomed well for Ms. Pearsall because she has taken the lemon of a market and made lemonade out of it. She has been able to purchase properties that would have been normally available for a higher asking price and purchased them for well under the market value.

This has allowed her to make good returns on her investments. Any businessman and woman knows that when you seek out potential investments, no matter what the business, you want to get a good return on your investment. Your return on investment (ROI) will determine whether or not you pursue a deal. Well, the deals that Ms. Pearsall have been making have been nothing but positive for her. Her strategy for her success has been to buy and hold her investments. She says, "she loves the idea of having someone to buy her property. Pay her a profit, and build equity in the property for her while the property appreciates over time".

Being a real estate investor has its perks says Ms. Pearsall. She enjoys her tenants and says that they feel blessed to have her as a landlord and she feels blessed to have them as her tenants. Making deals and making money without having to work so hard is what Ms. Pearsall loves doing these days. Ms. Pearsall also believes that you must have a plan when it comes to being a real estate investor. Her plan was to be financially free by the time she turned 34.

Well, in 2005 Ms. Pearsall made that dream a reality. She was able to quit her job and become financially free when her investment properties tripled what she was making on her job.

She says, "you cannot put a price on freedom, the sky looks bluer". Her investments are in Baltimore and North Carolina. Her intent is to not stop there either as she plans to do more investing in other states as well.

THE FUTURE

Growing her investment portfolio is what Ms. Pearsall intends on doing in the future. She also plans on writing other self-help books on real estate investing. Her first book, which she published is now available as well "Let Real Estate Work For You As It's Doing For Me". Ms. Pearsall believes in her pursuit of not only making herself financially free but also helping others achieve financial freedom as well. She talked about a real estate deal that she had tried to make for herself and wound up turning the deal over to a friend of hers. She says that she had a property (condo) that she had made an offer on. The offer was accepted and everything looked good until about a week before the deal was to go through. She says that the condo association wanted her to be an owner occupant of the property, which she did not intend on doing. She could not go forward with the deal and that is when she turned it over to her friend, who could live in the property.

She says that the best part about the deal she gave to her friend was that it turned into 5 deals. She says that she now owns 5 properties from Maryland to North Carolina. What Ms. Pearsall says that she learned from that experience is that you are blessed when you give, and after I blessed my friend with that deal the Lord Blessed me with 6 more deals. The more you give the more you receive, she says. With her unfailing determination Ms. Pearsall has put the real estate industry on notice that she will do things her way and in her time.

She gave an example of a deal that she was trying to make with a bank for a foreclosed home. She had put an offer that was well below the list price. She says, she went back and forth with the bank and was getting no where. She says she then decided that she would make her last and final offer and would put an expiration time and date on it. When her agent saw she had done this she told her that she could not do that.

180

Her agent told her that she had worked in the industry for many years and this had never been done. Her offer was to expire that day at 3:00pm. She went about her day and at 2:59pm she received a call from her agent letting her know that she had just received the signed contract from the bank. Now that is what I believe is making a mark in your industry. Never let anyone tell you that it can't be done. The truth of the matter is when you believe in yourself and you have everyone else telling you something to the contrary stay with what you feel. This would not be the only time that Ms. Pearsall would prove herself to be the savvy businesswoman that she is.

She has in the past year closed on two properties on the same day and with the same attorney. Many of us know how difficult it is to complete one business deal in a day and she closes two. All I can say to that is you go girl! Many a businessman and woman could learn a thing or two from Ms. Pearsall. Well, that will not be hard to do since she also goes around and speaks at churches and real estate investor meetings. She has been a speaker at seminars as well as been featured in Black Enterprise in a couple of issues. She loves reaching back to others and helping them get where they want to be financially. She is also the recipient of the 2006 Investor of the Year award.

As you prepare to make your journey into entrepreneurship or to continue in your purpose of being an entrepreneur, know that it does not matter where you start but what are you willing to do to finish. Ms. Pearsall is running her race and does not have to worry about sitting across from Donald Trump and him saying those two words from "The Apprentice". What Mr. Trump better worry about is Ms. Pearsall sitting across from him and telling him "Deal Or No Deal".

CHAPTER 17
FEEDING YOUR MIND
(WITH A GOOD BOOK)

JULIE WILLIAMSON

OWNER
A GOOD BOOK BOOKSTORE

INTRODUCTION

For me nothing is more exciting than to pick up a book and get entangled in the author's words. From poetry, to business, to autobiographies, to spiritually up lifting text. Each year for the past several years I have set a goal for my self to read books that have an affect on different aspects of my life. I like to read books on business and finance to keep me abreast of things that are going on in my professional life. I like to read spiritually fulfilling books that feed my soul. I like to read books that are personal biographies so that I can learn about interesting people's lives. I also like to read books that are about love and relationships as well as politics and societal issues.

The reason that I do this is because my goal is to be a well-rounded person. Just as the music that I listen to crosses different genres, and just like my church involvement addresses different aspects of my life, I apply the same logic to reading books. There is something enticing about reading a novel that is well put together and keeps you wanting to turn to the next page.

When you are reading a good novel it can have you up all night. I remember reading this one book by a well-known author and the book got so good that I could not put it down. I found myself up until about 1 or 2o'clock in the morning just so that I could finish this book. I found myself trying to make time during the day to read this book so that I could finish it. That is what reading a good book will do to you.

I enjoyed reading a book about the billionaire Robert Johnson, and how he came to be the businessman that he is today. I was spellbound by Candice Dow's two novels Caught In the Mix, and Ain't No Sunshine. I have been spiritually up lifted by Dr. Miles Monroe, Bishop T.D. Jakes, and Bishop Walter S. Thomas. I have had my hormones touched by a few of Zane's novels, those who have read her know what I am talking about! I have been enlightened by the great mind of Dr. Cornel West, and I have been encouraged by personal stories like Ms. Sandra Pearsall. All of these books and individuals that I have mentioned have fed my mind. They have helped to increase my vocabulary and have also helped me to increase the knowledge that I have. The books have expanded my thinking process and even helped me to understand some things that were going on in my life.

When I looked to find these books I could have gone to any bookstore that I wanted to. I could have even gone online and ordered them. What I wanted to do was to find a bookstore that was specifically owned and operated by someone that looked like me. I also wanted to support another business that was like mine.

What I mean by a business like mine is that it was an independent small business that was trying to make its mark like I was. I have seen a couple of black owned bookstores come and go in the Baltimore area. I recently noticed that there was one particular bookstore that opened in the Owings Mills Mall, which is located not very far from where I live. This bookstore was not in the mall much longer than a year. I started to ask myself why were the independent bookstores falling prey to the larger chain bookstores. Was it some super power that the bigger chain stores possessed that allowed them to gain more customers? Was it the ambiance that you got when you walked into the store? Or was it just the name?

After pondering this for a while, I sat back and thought about where I could find the answers. In my search to find those answers I came across a quaint little bookstore located in a small part of the Baltimore/Woodlawn area. I came across this bookstore and its owner by way of an email. The email gave me information about having the opportunity to network with other entrepreneurs and to discuss our businesses and business strategies. When I went to visit the bookstore I was first impressed with the atmosphere that was created in the store. I was impressed because I have not been in any other bookstore that makes you feel warm and welcome.

The other thing that caught my attention was that the owner of the store was out talking to some of the customers and also took the time to talk with me. I surely do not get that when I go into any of the big chain stores. The bookstore had a family feel to it and that was just the thing that made it special to me. After perusing the different books in the store and talking with the owner I wanted to come back again and again, and I even told others about this bookstore. The focus of the bookstore is one of knowledge and giving those who might not otherwise get the opportunity to showcase their literary talents. This bookstore gives the local author the opportunity to shine where the big chains only want authors who already have a name. They forgot that they once started off small too. This place is a place where you will find knowledge, wisdom, and encouragement. On the corner of hope and inspiration you will find owner Ms. Julie Williamson and **A Good Book Bookstore.**

BEGINNINGS

This Jamaican native learned early how to work hard. Moving here when she was just five years old, Ms. Williamson said that she learned how to work hard from her parents. She says that it was instilled in her that you worked hard and went to school so you could get a good job. Once she finished high school Ms. Williamson entered the Army and spent the next four years serving this country as a payroll specialist. After serving her country she entered the civilian world and continued performing payroll and accounting duties for companies but found it very dissatisfying. Ms. Williamson says that she has always wanted to start her own business but was unsure of what that business would be. She says that she started by doing things like selling jewelry, perfume, and even got involved in multi-level marketing. After trying these other forms of entrepreneurship Ms. Williamson says that she found what she thought was her passion, desktop publishing.

She would do that for a while for a company and then would venture off on her own and would become an independent contractor for a company by the name of 24-hour secretary. She spent the next 8 years doing that until it became to frustrating to deal with. Ms. Williamson says that between getting carpal tunnel and the dead lines it was too stressful.

After getting out of the desktop-publishing industry Ms. Williamson says that she took an interest in real estate. At the time the real estate market was doing very well so she become a loan officer. She felt that this would be better than becoming an actual agent. She also felt that being a loan officer gave you more independence. She says that the company that she decided to go with allowed you the opportunity to open your own branch, hire your own employees and run it as your own business. As she got more experience as a loan officer she learned more about the real estate industry and saw that the market was growing. She took full advantage of the growing market and began to invest herself. She would not do it alone though.

Ms. Williamson would get her family involved and would soon start her own real estate investment company. They purchased some properties in the Baltimore area. Ms. Williams says that things were going well with the loans, and with the investments, which created positive cash flow for her. Even with the other business ventures Ms. Williamson still wanted more. She says that she wanted a business of her own. She is an avid reader so she said she began to read books that talked about finance, retirement, and wealth building. What she says she got out of those readings was that you must have multiple streams of income.

She began to see that there was a difference between being self-employed and a business owner. She wanted to be a business owner, something that was hers, she says. Ms. Williamson would take the books that she read to heart and would set out to create her own multiple streams of income. Her plan, which I think any good business minded person would take heed to, is to be self-employed, a business owner, and invest. She says that she had the self-employment and investment aspect of her plan in place and that would leave the last piece of the puzzle to put into place and that was becoming a business owner. She still was unsure of what type of business it was that she wanted to own. There are many of us who go through a period of finding what our niche or talent is, and we all must keep going until we find it. This life that we live has a purpose and a destiny. It is not until we fulfill our destiny and walk in our purpose that we find our desire and passion.

Ms. Williamson would soon find her purpose. She is a subscriber of Black Enterprise magazine, which I believe every black business owner should subscribe to. She read an article on a new bookstore that was opening in New York, and would be inspired from it and would begin her research on becoming a bookstore owner. She got excited about the idea and would use the internet to gain access to information about opening a bookstore.

Ms. Williamson says that the first website that she went to was fabjob.com, which is a website that gives you information about different careers and industries. She found a book that she thought would put her on her way to entrepreneurship and once she received it she would be on her way. She says that the deeper that she got into her research the more confidence that she gained in believing that she could accomplish her goal. Let that be a lesson to all of us who think that a business will just fall into our laps. You have to do your research before you can accomplish anything in business. You must also have a plan.

After doing her research Ms. Williamson would come to the next level of becoming a business owner and that would be figuring the cost to become an entrepreneur. She calculated what it would cost her to open her awaiting bookstore. Once she figured out how much she needed then she had to figure out where the capital would come from to start her business. Ms. Williamson would not go the traditional route to raise her capital. Since she had multiple streams of income she would pull from one of her other streams, that being an investment property that she had equity in, and would use the money in that property to gain access to the capital that she would need in order to open her own bookstore.

In this day and time we have to be creative in how we gain access to capital. You can use non-traditional means to open a business but be sure to have a plan as Ms. Williamson did. With her non-traditional capital Ms. Williamson was on her way to opening her bookstore. Doing her due diligence Ms. Williamson would locate a quaint little area located in Baltimore's Woodlawn area. It is a small business district that suited her and her taste very well. As a business owner one of the keys to having a successful business is location. When you have the right product in the right area it is a formula for success. Ms. Williamson had found her perfect match for her vision.

THE INDUSTRY

Our economy is shrinking. While there seems to be an increase in mergers of major corporations, the bigger corporations seem to be putting the smaller companies out of business. This economic shrinkage is occurring in most industries today. The bookstore industry is no different than any other industry. It has its cycle just as any other industry.

Ms. Williamson says that "her industry is not an industry that you make a lot of money in unless you have a chain". The modern day independent bookstores are equivalent to the earlier day mom and pop stores that used to be in our communities. There are not many black owned bookstore chains so the majority of them are independently owned and operated. Many of them have also closed their doors.

Ms. Williamson has set out to prevent her doors from closing like some of the other bookstores that have been in the Baltimore area. Her passion and desire to disperse information will aid her in achieving her goal. Separating herself from the other bookstores that are in this industry today is what makes this bookstore owner very unique.

She has set out to bring people from a world of ignorance to world of knowledge and progression. Her bookstore offers books that focus on self-help and giving individuals access to information. Taking a page out of Home Depot's philosophy, "you can build it, we will help you", she is enlightening and empowering individuals to gain knowledge and to use that knowledge to live a better life.

She offers books that touch all aspects of individuals' lives. She says that if you want to get your finances in order, they have books on that, if you want to get your spiritual life together they have books on that as well. She also has books that will aid you in getting your relationships in order. Ms. Williamson says that whatever aspect of your life that you want to make better she wants to offer books that will aid you in that process. The energy and atmosphere that comes from this young entrepreneur's bookstore is rare in this day and time.

What Ms. Williamson and A Good Book gives you is an intimacy that cannot be felt in her counterparts or the big chain stores. As Ms. Williamson puts it "at a Good Book the customers will know me, the owner, I am not behind the scenes. I am actually at the cash register ringing up customers". She says that her customers leave her store with what they came for or knowing where to get it.

When you walk into the bigger chain stores there is a coldness that goes unnoticed by the average bookstore consumer, but for those of us who like the family atmosphere, intimacy, and friendliness you would be doing yourself a great favor by going to A Good Book. In many industries today there is a disconnect between the customers and the owners. When you can connect with your customers on an intimate level you can better meet and exceed their expectations.

The more that you meet or exceed the expectations of your customers the more people will want to visit your establishment or use your product or services. Many business owners have forgotten what their customers look like. They do not take the time to get to know their customers on an intimate level. The better you know your customers the better you are able to anticipate their needs, know their likes and dislikes, understand what they want, and you will be able to serve them better.

The gap between owner and customer is getting wider. It is getting wider because business owners have taken their focus off of the customers and have put it on their bottom line. When a business focuses more on their bottom line rather than its customers it more than likely will not be successful. Once we as business owners begin to go back to the basics of business, which is getting to know our customers, we can begin to change the industries that we represent.

Ms. Williamson is on her way to representing her industry very well. She has carved a niche in an industry that looks to what is hot as opposed to offering crucial information to people that will have a positive impact on their lives. Ms. Williamson also says that slowly resources are becoming available to help the independent bookstore and keep them going.

Ms. Williamson says that the American Book Sellers Association (ABA) has a program that is specifically geared towards independent bookstores. She says that they have conventions; they work with publishers to help them get better deals. They also have resources on helping them to get more education on selling books. She says that the ABA is there to help independent bookstores stay in business. Ms. Williamson says that the industry today is heading in a positive direction. One thing that she mentioned is that the change in the ISBN number going from 10 digits to 13 digits is an indication that more people are writing books.

She also says that there are more people are self-publishing. The self-publisher needs the independent bookstores says Ms. Williamson. They need us because the major chains do not promote most self-published authors into their stores. The independents give self-publishers the opportunity to promote and get their books in the market. Ms. Williamson and A Good Book is a big promoter of self-published authors.

She has had several events in her store that specifically cater to self-published authors. I recall visiting her store for the "Extravaganza" she had that featured a list of authors who were able to talk about their books and read exerts from them so that people could get a feel for what their books were about. She has also had authors who were signed to the larger publishing companies do book signings. She has had Candice Dowe, Zane, and Bernadette Stanis (Thelma from Good Times), just to name a few authors who have graced A Good Book with their presence.

Ms. Williamson is also an advocate of local authors. She wants to give them the opportunity to shine and become well known authors. She says that local authors are really not supported in the industry and need to be given the opportunity to get their books out.

THE FUTURE

Moving forward in this New Year Ms. Williamson and A Good Book is poised to help individuals do better - help them to do better spiritually, financially, and physically. So many of us do not take the time to educate ourselves on things that have an affect on our lives. Working in the clothing retail industry I learned that so many men, both young and old were not taught about the clothes that they wear.

They would come into the store and not know their suit jacket size, or know their waist size, or their neck size; some were not even taught how to tie a tie. What is significant about what Ms. Williamson and A Good Book is she is preparing people for their future. The more knowledge that people have the better equipped they are to handle life.

In this 21st century we have access to a lot of information and that information needs to be used more often. Many of us do not want to take the time to search for information that can be critical to us moving to the next level. We are so caught up in this microwave mentality, and thinking that we have to have everything right now. Once we realize that we have to work for everything that we get his will help us to endure those disappointments that we will go through. Information is the key to us moving forward.

Ms. Williamson is keen on giving others information and letting others know what is available for them. Getting people to realize what they have access to is what you will get when you enter A Good Book bookstore. Ms. Williamson is looking to open another location. There is a wealth of information stored in the books that sit on the shelves of this small but powerful business. This bookstore will take you places that you never thought that you would be able to go. You will be taken from high places to low places.

You can find out how people lived their lives and moved their lives from the valley to the mountain. You can discover who you are and where you are going, if you so desire. Your soul can be healed, your body can be changed, and your mind can be uplifted all in this one place. Where you go and what you do is up to you. The path has been paved and the course has been drafted. All that awaits is for you to take the first step towards your journey. As Ms. Williamson says, "Your journey awaits you at A Good Book".

CHAPTER 18
GENERATION - WE ARE NEXT

FARAJII MUHAMMAD

CO-FOUNDER
NEW LIGHT LEADERSHIP
COALITION INC.

INTRODUCTION

Brother Farajii R. Muhammad is a young leader, student, and dynamic speaker from Baltimore, Maryland. At the age of 19, Farajii co-founded New Light Leadership Coalition, Inc. and currently serves as the President and spokesperson for the youth governed organization. Brother Muhammad has 8 years of experience working with youth in the community and has served as the Youth Minister at the Nation of Islam's Muhammad Mosque Number Six in his hometown.

A passion for voicing the concerns of the youth have led him to many avenues including speaking at community events, presenting workshops at conferences across the country, and interning at Baltimore City Hall. Farajii hosted Makes Me Wanna Holla, a youth talk radio show on Baltimore's WBGR 850AM and appeared every Wednesday with "Reality Check" on Day Break with Anthony McCarthy, the first morning news show on Morgan State University's WEAA 88.9FM in Baltimore.

He is currently the host of Listen Up! With Farajii Muhammad, airing every Monday at 6:00pm on WEAA 88.9FM. Listen Up! is about going behind the news and straight to the issues by dialoguing with local newsmakers and national headliners about politics, education, health, finance and more, while always keeping young people in mind.

Farajii is currently a graduating senior at Towson University studying Mass Communications and Public Relations. He has also attended Baltimore City Community College and was honored on the 2001 National Dean's list for his academic achievements.

Back in the day when I was growing up in the city of Baltimore, my friends and I would go down to the nearby elementary school to the basketball court. We would talk a whole lot of a trash and brag about what we were going to do to the person that would be guarding us. We would sometimes go first thing in the morning and would not return home until the sun went down. There were times that we would have to wait at the court because there were fellas already playing on the court. When this would happen, we would call out when we got to the court We Are Next! Letting everyone know that we would be the next team that would take on the winner of the ongoing game.

In this ongoing game that we as young entrepreneurs are in there is a new generation of entrepreneurs that are saying We Are Next! They are excited, enthusiastic, ambitious, relentless, purposeful, and will not be denied. Although there are many who will try to silence them and try to keep their voice from being heard, they are not having it. They will not be ignored, they will not be denied, and they will achieve greatness no matter what the cost. They are visionaries, creative geniuses, political pursuers, financial go-getters, business movers and shakers, and worldwide wonders. They are our future. They will be the ones that our generation looks to too take care of us when we get older, Wow! What a thought. They are eager, anxious, and poised to take their turn at this world and see what it has to offer. They are stepping up to the challenge as young David did when he faced Goliath. They are ready to take their place as the one who will be counted on to move us into the next century.

They refuse to be put into a box and will not be confined by the traditional way of thinking. Their strategies may be unorthodox, and their tactics untraditional but they still long to get the same results. They want to be heard, they will be heard, and they must be heard. I met a young gentleman who is a part of this generation of budding entrepreneurs and was in awe at what he had to say. This young gentleman has a voice in his community and is using it to bring others like himself to the forefront of that community to show that they have a voice. Meet the voice of generation We Are Next. Mr. Farajii R. Muhammad and the **New Light Leadership Coalition, Inc (NLLC).!**

BEGINNINGS

This Baltimore native got his beginning in the city that "believes". He is a product of the Baltimore city school system as well as the school of the arts. As Brother Muhammad puts it, "he went to the school of the arts to become the next Denzel Washington". Brother Muhammad had a good childhood as he puts it. He grew up in and around the Nation of Islam of which he is still apart of today. His mother passed away from cancer when he was just 10 years old. He says that from that point on he continued to grow. He had an older brother and sister who would leave the nest before him and leave just he and his father in the household. He says that his father taught him how to be a young man of principle, and integrity. He serves as the Youth Minister for Mosque number six in Baltimore, Maryland. At the age of 18, Brother Muhammad went to Chicago to live with relatives.

Brother Muhammad says that his uncle Jackie also played an important role in his life. He says that he was the one who taught him how to get acclimated to a new environment, business, truth, honesty, and discipline. Brother Muhammad cherishes the relationship that he had with his uncle. There are not a lot of young men in our communities today who have a positive male figure in their life.

This is one of the most unfortunate things that exist in our communities today. We as entrepreneur men must pick up the mantle and set the example for our young brothers. I see so much on television, with Ms. Oprah Winfrey, and many other women of color in the position to be able to help other young women become strong women but I do not see the same emphasis put on our young men today. You cannot listen to the radio, read a book, or watch television without there some type of topic that deals with the specific issues of young women today. We have placed so much emphasis on our young women that we have left our young men by the way side and we are getting to the point where they feel hopeless.

It is up to us as the next generation of men to ensure that we put the focus on our young men to let them know that they have a voice and that someone cares about them. When we can build the next generation up to show them what it is to not only be strong men and women of character we also show them what it means to be great entrepreneurs. Who knows we could be raising the next Reginald Lewis, or the next B. Smith.

Brother Muhammad says that his uncle took him under his wing and really mentored him. He says that he gave him a book by Napoleon Hill, "Think and Grow Rich". He says that this book changed his thinking. His uncle taught him that in order to be successful you have to change your understanding, change your mind and change your attitude. Brother Muhammad says that he began to understand some of the things that his uncle had been teaching him but it really did not start to sink in until he came back home to Baltimore. He says that he started working and discovered that he was not someone who liked to punch a clock. Through this discovery would come a great blessing. He would come to meet his now wife Sister Tamara Muhammad, who is also in the Nation of Islam. He says that they began by having many conversations and would soon find out that they had a lot of the same ideas one that included wanting to do something for young people of today.

They went to the Millions Youth March in Atlanta and started on their journey to moving the youth of today forward. Out of their many conversations would come the brainchild, which is now the Organization that they began the New Light Leadership Coalition, Inc.

The organization is geared to the development of youth leadership. Brother Muhammad says that the first thing they did as an organization was put together a national conference at Douglas High School, which attracted about 100 students from the Baltimore/DC area. This was done mind you without any type of funds available for them accept for their own. Since the conference was so successful, they began to have it on an annual basis and have held it annually since 1999. The organization was built around the conference that they held. From the conference, they would branch out to also offer training for the youth. They would develop the youth leadership development program. The program would be a curriculum that was based on their experiences in learning the different areas of leadership. Those areas include social, political, technology, and organizational development. The philosophy of their organization is that if young people see other young people in leadership positions then they are more inclined to learn and listen.

Brother Muhammad also says that the philosophy of the New Light Leadership Coalition is that here is a young person and there is another young person. He is in a position where he can be a part of the decision making process. He is in a position where his leadership can influence others. He says that he is able to bring those others into the same position that he is in. Brother Muhammad and his wife Tamara did not have much of a guide to go by when it came to organizations like theirs. When they did their research about youth organizations they found that there were not many that did what they were trying to do.

Brother Muhammad explained to me the difference between a youth organization and a youth governed organization is that a youth organization is an organization that is run or could be run by adults who have a passion for youth; where as a youth governed organization is an organization that is run solely by youth. In the spirit of this organization it is all about the youth. It is an organization that is for youth run by youth. There is a lack of focus on the youth in general today. I say this because when you look at the condition of our public schools, when you see recreation centers closed down, when you see that there is no concerted effort to engage our youth in activities that will stimulate their minds instead of them just sitting countless hours in front of the television, what do they have to look forward to.

We wonder why our youth are disinterested in what is going on in the world today. It is because we are not involving them in the process and that process is called life. They cannot learn about life in front of a television or playing video games, and they surely cannot learn about life watching a video on MTV. There is someone, who is trying to change the mindset and mentality of our youth and that is Mr. Farajii Muhammad and the New Light Leadership Coalition.

THE INDUSTRY

The non-profit sector of business is in need of an overhaul as well as many of our businesses. They are in need of younger men and women who would be able to bring a rejuvenation and innovativeness to organizations that are getting older by the year. There are some organizations that have been around for many years and they have had the same people in the same positions for many years.

One thing that strikes me in the business community is the lack of older businessmen and women grooming some younger man or woman to take over the organization when they are ready to step down. I read an article about a certain organization that has been around for many years and the leader of this organization has taken ill.

The leader has had to step back from his position and the day-to-day activities so that he can recover from what is ailing him. The organization has in place a board to handle the day-to-day functions of the business but they do not have anyone like the leader ready to take his place while he is out as well as when he is ready to step down for good.

Not having someone ready to step into the shoes, as a leader is becoming an all too familiar scene today. Many of these organizations will find themselves fading out if they do not prepare for their future by preparing the young men and women of their perspective businesses to take over. Many of our youth today are not prepared for leadership. They are not prepared for leadership because many of our older generation have counted them out. Our government has counted them out, and many in our communities have counted them out.

There is a serious gap between the older generation and the younger generation. That gap is getting wider every year. Our seniors are getting to retirement age and the businesses that they run will have no one to take over if we do not begin to close the gap between the older and the younger generation.

I recently spoke with an older gentleman about his wife who has her own business that she has been running for 28 years. He proceeded to tell me that his wife has such a difficult time getting good hard working individuals for her company. His wife will be looking to be able to retire pretty soon and the woman that she has as her assistant is not equipped to take over the organization or run the day-to-day operations.

This younger woman is not showing any initiative in wanting to move up to take over the day-to-day operations for whatever reason. If she were then the gentleman's wife might be inclined to take her under her wing and groom her to take over.

Leadership cannot be forced on anyone. You must want and desire it. I do not believe that it is something that you are thrust into. I believe that you either are a leader or you are a follower.

Our younger generation is desirous of learning. They are looking to the older generation to take them into the positions that they once held. There is something special about seeing a young person who is willing to step up and make his or her voice heard. There have been few in history who have taken on the leadership banner at a very young age. In this day and time there are many more who would relish at the opportunity to be leaders if they were given the chance. Developing young leaders starts with a renewing of their minds.

The renewing of their minds begins with education, formal and informal. We must first teach them who they are. They must understand where they come from, and they must understand where they are going. This is a new era that we live in. We have to use non-traditional means to reach a non-traditional generation. We can no longer think inside the box. What we have done in the past does not work today so we must conform our thinking to be able to reach this new generation of leadership.

One such organization that is geared to reach that new generation of leadership is New Light Leadership Coalition, Inc.. The NLLC is geared to empower youth through a holistic, peer-centered approach to leadership development. The curriculum of the organization is not only based on its leader's experiences but they are also based on practical knowledge and guiding principles that can be used right now. Brother Muhammad says that they have a 164-page workbook that students can use as a guide for learning about the basic aspects of life. It shows them how to set up a bank account, how to apply for college, how to build up your credit, how to write a resume.

They also deal with learning about the political structure of our government, and organizational structure of companies. The skills that young people can learn from this workbook will help them in becoming young leaders.

Brother Muhammad said that they are finding that more and more young men and women are wanting to get involved in non-profit work. What has made Mr. Muhammad and his organization unique to others that are in this industry is that the organization is run totally by young people. As Mr. Muhammad mentioned earlier, when he talked about the difference between a youth oriented organization and a youth governed organization, NLLC is a youth governed organization and its Board of Directors are youth, and are in complete control of the organization. Brother Muhammad says that his organization is not trying to be like other organizations and be a one-stop shop. He says that their focus is on leadership training and that they try and do that best.

Their goal is one of prevention and not trying to do something after the fact. Growth and development is a key element to Mr. Muhammad and his organization. With growth and development comes a need for patience, he says. Many of our youth of today have what I call a microwave mentality when it comes to business or any other matter. They want things quick, fast, and in a hurry. They do not want to have to wait for anything.

The NLLC is an organization that will show the younger generation that if you are going to be a successful leader or entrepreneur then you will have to be patient. Many of us do not realize what it takes to be a leader or business owner. Most businesses do not make it past five years. Trying to get a successful business started can be very tiresome and very discouraging at times, but when you look at the big picture what is a couple of years to get a business to a level where it can flourish. Our youth have to learn to see beyond today. A lot of them do not look beyond today because they do not see themselves beyond that.

With organizations like NLLC there will be less young people thinking just for today and thinking about tomorrow and beyond. Brother Muhammad and his company are here to help youth see their end goal and to help them understand that with the struggles they will go through they will be able to persevere because they know that in the end what they are working for is something that is valuable.

Brother Muhammad and the NLLC exist to help surround the young future leaders with like-minded individuals. Brother

Muhammad believes that this is a key element in any entrepreneur's development. Having that familiar support around you, along with the love and support of others helps to make one successful. What the NLLC will offer young men and women from a customer perspective is "Professionalism" says Mr. Muhammad. Young people of today are not used to seeing other young men and women dressed in suites and ties, or women in business dresses and suits. Brother Muhammad says that when they are out at a speaking engagement and a young person sees them they will see them addressing people as sir or ma'am, they will show the young people respect as well as others.

Brother Muhammad says that with their leadership training they do not come in with the mindset that they are above the other young people in the program. They want the young future leaders to understand that they know where they are coming from and that they have been where they are. The NLLC has knowledge that they want to share with other young poised leaders such as themselves.

Brother Muhammad says that they do not want the other young people to feel left out. NLLC wants to make the youth feel as if their voice matters in society. There are not many organizations that are geared towards the young and the issues that they are dealing with today. There needs to be a concerted effort by organizations, whether in the public sector, or in the non-profit sector, to make the youth of today feel as if they are included.

In the non-profit sector culture, when a youth gets in a position of authority they abuse that authority. Some of those youth begin to believe the adults that try and pump their heads up, says Brother Muhammad. They begin to think that they are the greatest youth leader in the city. Brother Muhammad and the NLLC family are about respect, professionalism, and being humble, when it comes to serving the youth.

The NLLC unlike some other organizations are about creating a family atmosphere where youth are able to grow. When youth are taught by other youth they are more susceptible to learn says, Brother Muhammad. They can relate to the youth better than they may relate to their parent or an older person telling them something. Many adults were not and are not sure of this idea of youth teaching youth, because they did not feel that the older youth would be able to lead the younger youth. As Brother Muhammad put there was an uneasiness and distrust that the adults had. They felt there was no benefit in it.

Brother Farajii says that now, since their conference, there have been some who are receptive to the idea of the youth leading the youth. He says that it is still difficult getting the older generation to embrace this concept but they are seeing how well it is working. This new youth generation of leadership understands that you cannot use old means to reach the new generation of youth. This new generation of youth are so far advanced, brother Farajii explained. They have a creativity that is not like that of yesterday. The 11 year old of yesterday is not the 11 year old of today and the older generation has not figured a way to understand them on their level. The NLLC is geared towards understanding the new 11 year old and explaining things so they can understand it. A lot of the non-profit sector and individuals and industries in general are stuck on stubborn. They are stuck in their ways and are not willing to change it. If we are going to reach our youth it's time for change.

THE FUTURE

Change starts with a renewing of your mind. We in the black community have to begin to change our way of thinking. We are in a new time and era and if our focus does not begin to move in a new direction then we will continue to loose more of our youth. My mother and I had a conversation one evening and we were talking about the fight that her generation had and the fight that our generation is fighting. She told me that her generation had the fight of civil rights political entitlement and those barriers that held us back as a people. She said that our generation has a fight on a different level. The fight that we have is on an economic, financial, and technological. We have access to more resources than we have ever had before and we must begin to use the rights and access that our parents gave to us and begin to use it to create the economic leverage that our parents wanted us to have. The youth of today are so technologically advanced than our parents and they must use that to make the playing field level.

The youth of today must realize the power that is within them and take their rightful place in society and move us into the next

202

level of leadership. Brother Farajii sees the youth of today moving in the direction of creating more youth governed organizations. The non-profit sector will not only have more youth governed organizations but also stronger leaders than we have seen in the past.

The message that they are bringing is one of empowerment. There will be more emphasis on doing for self as opposed to relying on others to do for you, says Brother Muhammad. Since there is a lack of emphasis on our public school system and more of our youth are dropping out of school and going to jail. They will not be able to get a regular job because of the lack of education and their criminal record. Brother Farajii believes that this is forcing more of them into entrepreneurship.

Breaking away from the status quo and using non-traditional means to bring our youth into leadership and entrepreneurship is what we must begin to embrace. We have to revamp our educational system, which only has a graduation rate for young black men of 30% and a 57% graduation rate for girls. Something is wrong with that! We must begin to change those that are in the positions to do something about this or change the mentality of those who are in the position to make the necessary changes. Those in leadership positions must now be held accountable for the part that they are playing for not giving the youth of today access to a good education and the chance to succeed.

Changing the condition and the reality of the lives of our youth begins with strong leadership, says brother Farajii. He does not believe that the youth are dropping out because they do not want to learn, but it is what is being taught that is turning off the youth of today. What is being taught is old and the youth of today cannot relate to it on any level. There is a problem when you see more youth in the middle of the day on the outside of schools than you see on the inside of the schools.

We have to be more engaging, embracing and more compassionate towards our youth. It is no longer acceptable to be in a leadership position and not be a leader. The youth of today are learning that they must begin to have a clear understanding of what they want and how they can get it.

Brother Farajii Muhammad and the NLLC are poised to bring the youth of today into the forefront of our society and let their voices be heard. As brother Farajii said the real test is not to get something started, but to get everybody else excited about what you started. From the looks of things what Brother Muhammad and the NLLC has started has a lot of youth excited about being the New Generation of Entrepreneurs!

CHAPTER 19
STYLISH, SMART, AND SASSY

LOREZ ROBINSON REESE

PRINCIPLE
SIMPLY SAVVY EVENTS, LLC.

__INTRODUCTION__

Every little girl's dream is to grow up meet the man of her dreams, get married, and to spend their life happily ever after. Well, this is the real world that we live in and the reality is that may not happen.

In this day and time it has become the norm for people to meet get involved in a relationship, and to move on to the next one. I am someone who still believes in love. I believe that God has created someone for everyone. I believe that we should have someone that we share our lives with. There is nothing more special than knowing that there is someone who will support you when you are down, and celebrate with you when you are happy.

I had a friend of mine who lost both of his parents within six months of each other. I knew his parents and they had been married for over 35 years. In this day and time I know that this is a rarity but it is relationships like that that lets me know that happiness, love, and sincerity still exist in marriage today. To me there is something special about seeing two people in love. Seeing two individuals becoming one. I know that I am a guy and that guys are not supposed to be romantic but I have never been one to think like everyone else. I believe in love because I believe that God is love.

I cannot believe in a God who is the definition of love and not believe that he has created us in his own image and not have that love inside of us. We were created to love and to receive love. What I believe has happened in our society is that people have misused and abused the gift of love and it has caused many to not believe in it anymore.

We live in such a hurtful society that people have replaced compassion, and passion with callousness and abrasiveness. Getting people to show their vulnerable side is not an easy task. When you can get through the many facades that people show you, you may begin to see who they really are. Growing old with someone is about getting to know someone. As the years go by you should be learning more and more about that individual. You begin to learn their different mood swings, you see the character that is within them and you can hopefully move towards one of the most memorable days in your life, your wedding day.

I went to a book release party a few days ago. It was the first time that I had ever attended one of these events so I did not know what to expect. As I walked inside I was greeted by a hostess who directed me to where the party was being held. When I entered the room I was immediately taken by the atmosphere that was created by the dimly lit room and the smooth R & B music that played in the background.

There was a bartender who was attending to the needs of the guests sitting at the bar, and the waitresses were attending to the individuals that were scattered around the room. The mood had been set so that the guest of honor, an author that I am proud to know and is a fellow UMES HAWK, could sign books and ensure that everyone would have a good time. There were also individuals that were walking around with t-shirts that had the name of the book on them and there were bookmarks, and post cards of the newest novel by the author placed at each table.

The atmosphere was right, the music was tight, and the food was a delight. This author had put together an evening that I am sure will stay with her forever. Everyone that was in attendance seemed to be enjoying themselves and we all wished the author much success on her latest project. I am not sure if this book release party was this author's first one but I am sure that it will not be her last.

As I walked around the dimly lit room and sat at one of the corner seats, I took in the ambiance and thought to myself what I wanted my book release party to be like. I imagined people coming into a well-lit room, and being greeted by the host and hostess. They will be given a copy of "Young & Gifted, The New Generation Of Entrepreneurship", and they will be directed to either side of the room, which will have the entrepreneurs waiting to talk about their businesses and how they became the person they are today. There will be a great mixture of Jazz, and R & B music playing to keep the mood upbeat and flowing. There will be light food served to ensure that everyone is full and attentive.

There will be tables of information so that those in attendance will go away with more information than they came in with. The atmosphere will be filled with good food, good music, and some laughter. All with the back drop of inspiration and purpose.

When I thought about putting something like this together I knew that I could not do something like this, but I would soon come to know someone that could bring what was going around in my mind to reality. She specializes in making wedding days into forever memories, and corporate events into extravaganzas.

She can turn an ordinary event into something breathtaking. She is someone who will blow you away with her event planning talent, and her love for taking your event and turning it into something that is unbelievable!!! She is sexy, sassy, and savvy. She is Ms. Lorez Robinson Reese of **Simply Savvy Events, LLC.**

BEGINNINGS

This Brooklyn, New York native grew up the oldest child in her family. Her schooling would come from the Catholic and public school system. There is much to be said about having both a private and public school education. She says that from elementary school through middle school she went to school with the same kids. She says that this was important to her because she knew each year that she would see the same friends in school and they all grew up together. They were together from grade 1 through grade 8. Ms. Robinson Reese says that her Catholic school up bringing also gave her the foundation that she has in the Lord. She says that she grew up with her grandparents and great-grandparents, who raised her and her siblings, because her parents passed when she was young. She says that her grandparents and great-grandparents gave her

207

strong family values and really showed her what family was all about.

Ms. Robinson Reese says that her great-grandfather really showed her what being a business owner was about at a very young age. He was an entrepreneur and she says that had a great influence on her and helped to plant the seeds of entrepreneurship early on in her life. Her family would instill in her the core values that she still holds tightly to and has passed them down to her children. This is something that is missing in a lot of families today. Parents are not taking the time to give their children the values, morals, and responsibility that we had when we were growing up.

We saw it back then as our parents being mean, spiteful, and down right evil, but today we realize what they gave to us was more valuable than anything. Ms. Robinson Reese believes that it is important to have family and others around you who are supportive of your vision. She and I agree that there is nothing worse then being around people who do not have a vision.

When you are surrounded with like-minded individuals it is something that inspires you to work harder. You get insights that you might not otherwise have had if you were not around these people. I know being around individuals such as Ms. Robinson Reese is truly inspiring because of her visions and what she is about. I believe that as adults we are greatly influenced by the way that we grow up, and I can tell by being around Ms. Robinson Reese that she holds dear to her, her family and the things that were imparted to her as a young girl.

After high school she attended a local college in New York and earned her Bachelor's degree in Business Administration. Ms. Reese Robinson believes that college gave her a good foundation but did not completely prepare her for entrepreneurship. As with many colleges of my generation they did not have classes specifically geared towards entrepreneurship, while today a lot of colleges have courses and even an entrepreneurship major. I believe that this will greatly help those young adults, who are in college to go further along in their entrepreneurship journey than when we came out of school. Once Ms. Robinson Reese finished school she would do what most of us do, which is get a job working in corporate America. She entered the rat race as we all have done at one point in our lives and started on her career path and found herself wanting more. While she was first enthusiastic and energetic about doing Human Resources and the responsibilities that came along with it she says that she really began to feel like she did not fit in.

Ms. Robinson Reese is not one to play the corporate games that they want you to play in order to move up in a company. She was hard working and was good at what she did, but those of us who have chosen not to play the game know that is not enough. Part of the responsibility of being in Human Resources is that you plan the different company events. You plan the company picnics, the Christmas party, and any other special events. Well, Ms. Robinson Reese found herself planning these events and soon discovered that she had a knack for it. Well, I would say that she has had more than a knack for planning corporate events and weddings because that initial planning would be her start on the path to entrepreneurship. Ms. Robinson Reese worked for another company in Human Resources and found herself again planning the events for the company. She says that she just could not get away from it. Her ability to organize an event was evident from the beginning.

Ms. Robinson Reese says that "it is like putting the pieces of a puzzle together". Well, putting the pieces to her wedding puzzles has been nothing short of extraordinary for her and the Simply Savvy Events family. Ms. Robinson Reese said that her Simply Savvy Events Company came to reality while she was attending a wedding. She was at a wedding of some friends and she says that while she was attending the wedding there was all this chaos going on.

She says that the DJ did not have the correct songs, and a whole lot of other things were just totally out of order. She says that she stepped right in because she was quite familiar with doing these types of events and after the wedding she had one of the guests ask her if she would do the planning for her wedding. From that mishap at a wedding was born Simply Savvy Events, LLC. Ms. Robinson Reese says that the wedding that she would do was not an easy one by any means. It was a wedding that took place at a church on a Saturday evening in the sanctuary of the church that had to be broken down and set back up for service the next day. Ms. Robinson Reese says that after the event was over with and all of the breaking down and setting up was done, she was tired, but she loved it! It is truly something when you are doing something that you love to do and people will pay you to do it.

THE INDUSTRY

There are not many industries that will allow you to be as creative and as freewheeling as event planning. Now of course your clients will come in and tell you what they have in mind for their event but they will also depend on you to be as innovative as you can. If you are a painter you can be as abstract as you want to be. If you are a writer you can be as free flowing with your words as you want to be. If you are a musician you can be as out of the box as your imagination will take you. This is the same concept that this young entrepreneur takes when it comes to doing an event brought to you by Simply Savvy Events, LLC. Ms. Robinson Reese says that when she sits down with a client she aims to do something that no one else has done before.

Ms. Robinson Reese and myself share the same Pastor/Bishop so we understand what it means to give something extraordinary to our clients. Our Bishop has taught us through his ministry that you must be able to give your customers something new and fresh each time that you gain one so that their experience is something that they will not get anywhere else. I know when you hire Simply Savvy Events, LLC to do an event for you, you can expect an event that will not only meet your expectations but will exceed them.

Ms. Robinson Reese's definition of customer service is "understating what you will do and exceeding what you actually give to your clients". Ms. Robinson Reese says that what she means by this statement is that you do not want to tell your customers that you can give them everything and then not be able to follow through with it. So many companies will promise that they will do this and give you that just to get the sale, but when it comes time to actually give you what you asked for they find every excuse as to why they were not able to get it for you. When I worked in the hospitality industry there were many salesmen who would promise companies all kinds of things just to get their business and then when the group would check in and they would not be able to get what they were promised they would holler and fuss at us instead of the salesperson. It never failed that while we were feeling the fury of the customer the salesperson was never around and could not be found.

When you deal with Simply Savvy Events, LLC. you will not have to worry about them telling you that they can give you something and it not be there. They are professional, courteous, and progressive, in everything that they do. You can bet if it has Simply Savvy's name on it then it will be done in the right way. Ms. Robinson Reese says that what separates Simply Savvy Events from others is that she takes the time to get to know her clients. She has a consultation with her clients so that she can get to know them.

Ms. Robinson Reese says she records the conversations so that she can go back and get inside of her clients minds and really try and understand what they want to get out of the event. She says that by sitting and talking with the clients you can get to know them on a personal level and be able to invoke their personality into the final product.

More businessmen and women need to understand their customers better. The more you understand about your customers the better you are able to not only meet their expectations but to exceed them as well.

It is no surprise that Ms. Robinson Reese and the Simply Savvy Events, LLC family are not only well versed when it comes to their customers but are also well versed in their industry. Ms. Robinson Reese makes sure that she keeps abreast of what is going on in the industry by attending seminars, conferences, as well as reading the latest magazines that help her to see her industry from a broader perspective. No one wants to do business with anyone who does not seem knowledgeable about their perspective industry.

When you deal with Ms. Robinson Reese, you will get someone who is intelligent, practical, and informed. She seeks to bring something different to each and every client that she deals with. What you will also get with Ms. Robinson Reese is someone who does not think inside the box. She is someone who is looking to use her creativeness to the events that her company put on.

Simply Savvy Events, LLC. is not your ordinary event planning company. They will ensure that your event has everyone talking about it when they leave. One of the things that makes Ms. Robinson Reese special from her counterparts' in the event planning industry is that she is not afraid to share information. She says that as businessmen and women we are so afraid to share information because they think that others are trying to steal business away from you. In the event planning industry just as many other industries today, people feel as if the knowledge that they have gained is only for themselves. When you are confident in yourself and your abilities you do not have to worry what someone else is doing because your work will stand on its own, and so far Simply Savvy Events, LLC is standing tall and strong.

Ms. Robinson Reese also says that her industry is steadily growing. She says with the influx of "reality" shows, which show people having these lavish weddings, people are wanting to be just like them. She says that people are being more forward in their thinking than they have in the past. They are open to doing things outside the norm and they look to Simply Savvy Events, LLC to give it to them.

Ms. Robinson Reese has no problem catering to the customer that has an unlimited budget to work with the customer that has a limited amount of funds. She has no problem accommodating her clients and can relate to anyone on any level. The event planning industry is headed in a positive direction. Just as with any industry the event planning business has its cycles. It is experiencing growth and does not show signs of slowing down anytime soon.

THE FUTURE

Since 9/11 Americans have been living in more fear than ever before. That tragic event has caused us to live on edge and has made people more stressed than ever before. It has also caused people to a certain extent to take a look at how they are living. Many people are beginning to understand that tomorrow is not promised and they have taken on the mindset that they must live life to the fullest.

Ms. Robinson Reese believes that people are looking at events such as weddings with a more serious attitude. She says that people want to make their wedding an everlasting memory and therefore they go all out. She thinks that event planning is benefiting from peoples new attitude towards this once in a lifetime event.

The wedding and event planning industry is steady and moving strong into the future. With companies like Simply Savvy Events, LLC setting the benchmark for the industry there is no doubt that brides, grooms, and businesses have one less thing to worry about when planning a social gathering.

As industries move into the 21st century they have to be able to go beyond the traditional and ordinary. When you are able to think non-traditionally then you will be able to take the limits off of what you are able to offer your clients. Ms. Robinson Reese and the Simply Savvy Events, LLC family is one such company that adheres to this non-traditional thinking. Ms. Robinson Reese told me of a client who wanted to have her wedding in a cave. Yes, I said cave.

Those damp cold places that you see on television and read about in books. She says that no one would have ever thought to have a wedding in a cave, but this client wanted to have her wedding in this cave. Ms. Robinson Reese says that this client said that she had always wanted to have her wedding in a cave since she was a little girl. Well, Ms. Robinson Reese's attitude was whatever she wanted that would be what she would get.

I am an out the box person as anybody else but in my wildest dreams I would have never come up with having a wedding in a cave. This client would give Ms. Robinson Reese the opportunity to go way outside the box with her thinking because anyone who would have a wedding in a cave is pretty much game for anything else that you might bring to the table.

This is also a testament to the skills and talents that Ms. Robinson Reese brings to the table. She is versatile in that she can go the traditional route with your event or she can go the non-traditional route and give you a wedding in a cave. Whatever way that you want it Ms. Robinson Reese and the Simply Savvy Events, LLC family will make it happen for you.

Ms. Robinson Reese and Simply Savvy Events, LLC Company are not just diverse in their ability to accommodate your savvy event taste. They can also provide you with budget management, vendor referrals, invitations, accessories, and etiquette advice. So as you can see Simply Savvy Events, LLC is capable of offering services that touch their clients in more than one way.

In these economic turbulent times it is even more crucial that companies offer more than one type of service. We have talked about this in previous chapters and it bears being repeated. When a company can offer a number of services it only strengthens the financial standing of that company. Simply Savvy Events, LLC is one such company that is not content on just offering one type of service. By offering a number of services they also broaden their customer base.

From the look of things Ms. Robinson Reese and the Simply Savvy family will be offering those services to their clients for a mighty long time. The next time that you want to relieve yourself of the stress and strain of planning a big wedding day, or you have a big office event that you just don't know how you will pull it off, stop, take a breath, relax, think sexy, think sassy, think savvy, then call Simply Savvy Events, LLC and watch all your worrying go away!

CHAPTER 20
MIND FOR JUSTICE

KIMBERLY M. THOMAS, ESQ.

OWNER/FOUNDER
THE LAW OFFICES OF
KIMBERLY M. THOMAS

INTRODUCTION

There was a show on television some time ago about this gentleman who started his own law firm. His firm was very small and he barely kept his practice going in the beginning. One of the characters on this show was an attorney that had a passion and desire to see the law up held for his clients. The actor played his role so well as this attorney that I have often said that if I were in trouble I would want to have him represent me. I know that the actor was only playing a character on a television show but the same passion, zeal, and fight that the actor put into his character is the same passion, and zeal that the actor put into acting. He was such a convincing person that he made you believe that he was actually an attorney who could represent you if you needed to get representation.

There have been several other individuals who stand out to me when it comes to someone showing a passion and desire for what they do. Will Smith did it in Ali, Jamie Foxx did it in Ray, and Denzel did it in Hurricane. Although these were characters that these actors played the passion that they had for there craft made those of us who watched them believe that they were these people. Many of us do what we do just to make ends meet. Then there are those of us who do what we do because we love what we do. We enjoy the intricacies of the craft that we have chosen to be a part of. I know when I was in college and I chose to major in Hotel/Restaurant Management I enjoyed the challenges that it brought to me on a daily basis. As I have grown in my career and now have begun a new journey, I have found a new and more impactful passion. I have a passion for creativity. I like having a vision and bringing that vision to life. I love enlightening, and empowering people. When you can have a positive impact in other people's lives it gives you a very special feeling inside that cannot be put into words. You cannot even imagine the joy you feel when you have invested in someone else's life and they are the better for it. I admire those individuals that have chosen to serve others in any capacity.

In my quest to find someone who has chosen to serve others in the legal field I was introduced to a young, passionate, intelligent, spirited, woman who believes in fighting for what's right. In November of 2006 I had a legal issue that involved some traffic violations that were erroneously given to me. The whole matter should have never happened but that is another story. Well, since the violations were very serious and I was going to fight the violations but it would require the assistance of an attorney if I was going to handle the situation the right way. I asked an acquaintance of mine if he knew of an attorney that I could talk to about these violations and possibly take my case. The acquaintance gave me the name and number of the attorney and I called her to discuss the situation that I was in. As I explained my situation to her and what took place she quickly explained to me what she could do for me. From our first conversation I have felt her passion for what is right.

She is someone who will fight for those who may not be able to fight for themselves. She believes that everyone deserves a voice. She chose to take on my case and gave me a voice that I might not have had if I had not hired an attorney. She made sure on the day of my case that my voice was heard. As many of us know our voices in this society can be silenced when it comes to the legal system. There are not to many of us who in some form or fashion have had to deal with the law. Whether it was a traffic violation that was given on the words of a state's attorney, or a case brought against you for some other reason. No matter the situation it is good to know that if you are in need of legal representation you have someone who is not afraid to fight for you and will ensure that your voice is heard.

She is an attorney that is not afraid to stand up against the system. She is someone that is not afraid to say that the system is wrong. When the system is leaning against you it's good to know that you have someone who will lean back for you against that system. I know that on that day in the courtroom when the system was leaning against me I had someone representing me

216

that was leaning back. To see this young dove of a woman one would not suspect that there was so much passion, and fight in her. Don't let the quiet demeanor fool you. She is a fighter and has a mind for justice. She is Ms. Kimberly M. Thomas owner and founder of **The Law Offices of Kimberly M. Thomas.**

Beginnings

This legal connoisseur began her humble beginnings in the city of Baltimore, Maryland. In her younger years she would attend John Paul Regional School from kindergarten through eighth grade. She would go on to attend the Seton Keogh High School for high school. Once she finished high school she attended the University of Maryland College Park from 1993-1994. Ms. Thomas says that when she first went to the University of Maryland she wanted to be a doctor. She says that she wanted to be a doctor ever since she was a little girl. She wanted to be able to help people, but she found that she would be able to help people in a different way. When Ms. Thomas discovered in her first semester in college the number of science courses and labs that she needed to take she to go on to medical school, she decided that being a doctor was not for her.

After attending the University of Maryland College Park from 1993-1994, Ms. Thomas returned to Baltimore and enrolled at Catonsville Community College. She attended college full time and worked full time. She completed three semesters at Catonsville Community College and enrolled at the University of Baltimore. At the University of Baltimore, her major was initially history and then in her final year she switched her major to Jurist Prudence, which is Pre-Law. Ms. Thomas graduated from the University of Baltimore, with honors, in May 1997.

In the fall of 1996, as her undergraduate career was coming to an end, she decided that she wanted to attend law school. She applied to take the LSAT. This is the standardized test that everyone who hopes to attend law school must take. After sitting for the LSAT, she began to look at her options for law schools to attend. After weighing her options, she accepted the offer of admission presented by the University of Maine School of Law. She said that attending school in Maine was something different then going up there for a visit.

While getting ready to go away for Law School Ms. Thomas would be introduced to her now husband, David E. Thomas. She says that he was a perfect gentleman from the first time that she met him. She moved to Maine, with David's love and support, and she attended the University of Maine School of Law. Ms. Thomas believes that a certain level of education is always important and you as an individual have to figure out what that level is. She also says that as long as you are willing to role up your sleeves and work hard you can be good at whatever you set your mind to. She would go on and attend the University of Maine Law School and would finish up at the University of Baltimore Law School.

Ms. Thomas took the Maryland Bar examination in the summer of 2000. In the fall of 2000, she began a judicial clerkship with the Honorable Roger W. Brown, Sr., a judge on the Circuit Court for Baltimore City. After completing her clerkship, Ms. Thomas briefly worked for a small law firm in Anne Arundel County, Maryland. While working in the law firm, she realized that she missed working in Baltimore City and missed practicing criminal law even more. Ms. Thomas applied to the Office of the Public Defender for Baltimore City. She gained invaluable experience during her time with the Office of the Public Defender.

Ms. Thomas became pregnant with her son Noah David while working for the Office of the Public Defender. After the birth of her son, Ms. Thomas decided to stay at home and take care of her son. She says that she went back and forth with her decision whether or not to return to the Office of Public Defenders because the people that she worked with were wonderful and she really loved her job. But, she said that every time that she laid eyes on her son she knew that she could not leave him.

Ms. Thomas handled an occasional small legal matter while at home with her son until she was approached by her cousin who worked for a company that needed a lawyer. She said she talked it over with her husband and he was behind her all the way. She would make it known to her newfound clients that she had a baby and that she was not leaving him. They were fully supportive of her and told her to bring him along. She packed little Noah up several days a week and together they would meet with the Client and handle office business.

Ms. Thomas says that eventually Noah reached the age where he would not be able to go with her into the office. So, her mother, Gloria, graciously kept Noah and made sure that Noah was cared for in a loving environment. This marked the beginning of her trek into entrepreneurship. Ms. Thomas says that as she began to get busier she thought about looking for office space. She says as she walked downtown she would take notice of the places that had office space available. She found a quaint little office located in downtown Baltimore that suited her just fine. She says that she chose to get the office space because she wanted to be able to take on more criminal cases, which is her first love.

THE INDUSTRY

Our justice system is tainted at best. Just a few weeks ago I remember hearing on the news of a 7-year-old boy being arrested and put in jail. Yes, I said jail. Not juvenile detention, not taken home to his parents but jail. He was arrested for pushing a mini bike down the street. It is true that it is illegal to ride a mini bike in the city but this young boy was pushing it up the street. The police officers that were involved did not take him home to his parents, but instead chose to take him and place him in jail. He was eventually released but he never should have been taken there in the first place. Has our justice system gotten so callous that they believe that it is ok to put a 7 year old into jail? I have seen some things that I just could not believe when it comes to the law and our justice system, but this one I just could not comprehend. From the Rodney King beating, to the many police brutality reports filed, to the unlawful arrests here in my hometown, our justice system has gotten out of control.

There is no accountability in our society today. Children do not want to be held responsible for their actions, athletes do not want to be held accountable for the things that the people they hang out with do, and our police force does not think that they have to answer for any unlawful doings that they do. The law was meant to protect and serve those of us in society who try to do right. It is also meant to ensure that those who do break the law are given a fair trial and made to serve their debt to society.

All of us have to be accountable for the actions that we take and the decisions that we make. Whether we get caught up by circumstance or we get caught up by the reality of our actions we will need someone who is capable of making sure that the law is upheld.

Each year there are many individuals that pass the bar exam and become attorneys. Some go on to work for law firms, some take positions with corporations, some take jobs in the public interest sector of law, like with the office of the Public Defender, just to name several options available in the legal field. Ms. Thomas chose to work for the Public Defenders office and developed her career from there. Working in the Public Defenders office allowed Ms. Thomas to practice criminal law, which she says is her fist love. Being an attorney is not an easy career path to journey. Ms. Thomas talked to me about the competitiveness that goes on within the industry. Although many industries are competitive being an attorney is not like most other careers. "When become a attorney licensed to practice law in Maryland, you have a license to perform a skill and service that the average person cannot perform. It is a privilege to practice law", says Ms. Thomas.

In the field of law just as with any other industry what people want is service. Ms. Thomas believes that at the end of the day that it's not about the office that someone has but the service that they provide. She believes that when her clients walk through her doors they want to know that what they are getting is Kimberly M. Thomas and not a whole lot of other things and at the Law Office of Kimberly M. Thomas you will get exactly what you came looking for, an attorney who is committed to service. You can get any attorney to represent you if you can cover their fees, but what you don't want is an attorney that will look at you as just another fee. You want someone that will see you as a human being and as a client and will respect and represent you to the fullest. Ms. Thomas prides herself on treating each and every client that she represents both as a human being and with respect. Ms. Thomas says that she learned this lesson early on in her career while doing her clerkship for the Honorable Judge Roger W. Brown, Sr. She says that he taught her from the first day she worked for him to be nice to people. She says that he told her it did not matter whether it was the person cleaning the floors in the building, a person that is in handcuffs, a lawyer or a judge, you should be respectful and nice to them.

Ms. Thomas and the Law Offices of Kimberly Thomas not only believe in being nice to people they believe in listening, being accessible, being interested, being prepared, getting her clients involved, and giving an answer. Ms. Thomas believes that you should be providing every client with this type of service, and this is what separates her from the many other Law firms that are out there. She explained to me that as an attorney you must listen to your clients to be able to understand what they need. You must be accessible to your clients because they may have questions. You must give an answer to your clients even if the answer is I don't know. You must be interested in your client's case so that you are involved to a certain extent and handling the cases is not just what you do. You must be prepared, and you must get the client involved, Ms. Thomas says. She also says that you must get the client involved because they should know what is going on.

Ms. Thomas believes that people will not understand what is going on if you keep the knowledge to yourself. I am a witness to Ms. Thomas and her law firm practicing what they preach. When she was handling my case she took the time to prepare me for what was going to happen in the courtroom. True to what she said, everything she had prepared me for went on in the courtroom. There are some law firms that might take the time to let their clients know what is going to happen or what is going on but there are many that do not take the time to make their clients aware of exactly what's happening. The Law Offices of Kimberly M. Thomas is one of those law firms that believes in keeping its clients aware. With Ms. Thomas and her law firm the client comes first. She believes that the client must be clear on any questions that they may have. Ms. Thomas said to me that if the client does not understand something than you say it again and again until they do get it.

Ms. Thomas believes that being a young entrepreneur in the law field gives her the opportunity to be and do things her own way. She says that by owning her own firm she is able to take the cases that she wants to take, and practice the kind of law that she wants to practice. Ms. Thomas also says that there is a lot of pressure on you when you are an entrepreneur but at the same time its all yours. She says that her work ethic is not like everyone else's and she is always thinking about what she could be doing for her clients. In an industry that can be filled with individuals that can be callous, and money hungry, its good to know that there is a firm that believes in working hard for its clients. When you work hard for those who you provide a service for it will show. No matter the industry or the company hard work is hard work and it shows when it is all said and done.

Ms. Thomas also talked about what makes her firm different from others is that she cares. She says that she knows that billing is important but you also have to be fair. She told me of a firm that she worked for that put pressure on her about not billing her required amount for a particular week. There are many firms that are all about the dollar but there is at least one firm that will work with you when it comes to being fair about their billing procedures. In a day and time that the number of criminal cases are on the rise, and the number of frivolous law suites are prevalent, it's good to know that there is a law firm that will handle your case with dignity, relentlessness, and compassion.

THE FUTURE

From the comfort of her home to a quaint little office in downtown Baltimore, Maryland, the Law Office of Kimberly M. Thomas is growing. This law firm that was started by a young woman who wanted to help people is spreading its wings and taking on the personality of its owner. It is a firm grounded in fight, perseverance, and respect. Building on these three distinct qualities that are apart of the character of its owner the Law Offices of Kimberly M. Thomas is well on its way to etching its mark in the practice of law. When Ms. Thomas first started her firm she had very little start up cost. She says that she only had an extra phone line in her home, and gas going back and forth to her corporate clients office, and her cell phone. Her approach to growth has been different from other entrepreneurs. As she told me she did not take out the business loan like many other entre-preneurs do when they first start out and as a consequence she has not had the instant debt that many others have in starting their business.

Ms. Thomas attributes her strategy to both her and her husband's belief in being debt conscious. Many entrepreneurs believe that they must run out and get all kinds of loans so that they can get their business up and growing. As a consequence they get into this tremendous amount of debt and cause themselves to be in over their head in debt even before the doors to their business opens. There is nothing wrong with going out and getting a small business loan to get your business off the ground, if that is the best thing for you to do. You must have a plan, and you must be willing to work that plan so that you and your business can be successful. Some of us, like Ms. Thomas, have chosen to grow our businesses with as little overhead as possible and allow our businesses to progress without constantly having to worry about owing money to someone. When you allow your company to grow in stages and levels you are able to take your time and allow your business to be groomed as it goes through its different stages. Just as a child progresses into adolescence and then into a young adult, and then into adult hood, your business should be allowed to do the same.

When we try to grow our businesses to fast we can over burden ourselves and also set ourselves up for failure if you are not prepared for growth. Entrepreneurship is about being on a journey and a journey is not about how fast you get through it but the process that you go through in getting to where you are going. Where Ms. Thomas and her law firm are headed is in a direction that will keep her on the journey of helping others for a very long time. As entrepreneurs we are ever evolving, and Ms. Thomas and her firm is no different. As she is growing and evolving so is her law firm. She says that her firm is growing into something that she never thought that it would grow into so far. As the Law Office of Kimberly M. Thomas moves forward into the future it's potential is wide open and is full of vigor for justice. Filled with spirituality, passion, and integrity, Ms. Thomas has taken the strong foundation given to her by her mother, the love and respect given by her husband, and the strength given to her by her son, and built a firm that is setting the bar for excellence at a very high level.

Getting to help others in the manner that she does gives Ms. Thomas great pride. She says that she gets to do something that not everyone can do, which is litigate, and that is something Ms. Thomas considers a privilege. She also does not get mixed up what she does with who she is. She says that being a lawyer is what she does not who she is. She says that when she goes home for the day she does those things that pertain to her home and not work. She is careful to always put family first. She puts her family first when it comes to leaving something behind. Ms. Thomas talked about how she had friends in law school whose parents own there own law firms and they were able to slide on into there parents firm once they finished law school and what she wants to do is to leave something that her son Noah can slide into if he desires. For any entrepreneur guidance and support are two of the most important things that you can have. If you are going to navigate through the journey of entrepreneurship there has to be someone that has gone through what you have gone through that you can go to and those that will support you in your vision.

Ms. Thomas has been blessed to have individuals in her life who have been there in ways that have guided her and supported her in every step along her journey. She admires the Honorable Judge Roger W. Brown Sr., for the guidance that he has given her ever since she did her clerkship in his office. She says that he has been like a mentor to her and she can bounce things off of him when she needs to. She says that his knowledge and experience has helped her tremendously and she holds dear to her heart how him and his family have welcomed her and her family into their lives. Ms. Thomas also says that she admires her husband. As she began to talk about her "David" a big smile comes across her face. She says that she loves the man that he is and she values that he has stayed true to her. She says that throughout all of the experiences that they have had he has been there from the beginning and has always encouraged her to "go and be". She says that he has always let her know that no matter what he was always going to be there and she loves that about him. She also admires her mother for her strength and supportiveness. She says that her mother has sacrificed so that she had the things that she needed in her life.

As the gavel comes down on another day for the Law Offices of Kimberly M. Thomas and all the calls that could have been made are complete, the court room is quiet and everyone has gone home its good to know that when tomorrow comes there is a law firm located in downtown Baltimore that is not apart of the talking generation but the doing generation. It is a firm that will fight for you, respect you, and make sure that when you leave that courtroom or her office, you can say as the judge said to her when my case was finished "good job counselor". I echo the words of the Judge and say good job counselor and thank you for not only fighting for me but thank you for fighting for those who may not be able to fight for themselves and thank you for having a mind for Justice.

CHAPTER 21
HART TIMES 2

TOUSSANT HART

SOLE PROPRIETOR
HEART TWO HART DAYCARE

<u>INTRODUCTION</u>

I have saved this entrepreneur for last. I put her last not because of any order of significance but because with this entrepreneur it's personal. So far I have brought to you young entrepreneurs that I know through school, church, or through other people. This entrepreneur I know personally. She was introduced to me a long time ago. We go way back! As a matter of fact I could tell you stories about her, just as she could tell you stories about me, but we'll save that for another time.

This young entrepreneur's love for children started at a very young age. She has always had that motherly spirit about her. It takes a special person to want to teach or to take care of children. Your patience must be long and you must be in good shape, because children will run you raged. Children are the most precious gifts on earth and when you have a love to take care of them and take part in their early development it is something special. Knowing that you played a part in a young person's life can mean something to you, and that is why this young entrepreneur does what she does. She enjoys the joy that the children bring to her life.

In her neighborhood her house is the house that all the children know that they can go to and feel like it is a home. She has no problem letting the children know when they do something right and when they do something wrong. In this day and time we lack adults who will let children know when they are doing something wrong. We do not have adults that will hold young kids accountable for their actions.

Children in this day and time need to see adults being adults and not acting like children. It pains me when I see a mother

227

who is trying to capture her youth by hanging out all times of the night and trying to be best friends with their kids. In today's time you can barely tell who is the child and who is the parent. Children are out of control and so are the parents. The children are not disciplined at an early age and therefore they feel as if they can do what they want to do when they get older. When you have babies having babies, the result is chaos and disorder. That disorder is leading to destruction.

As I see young parents loosing control of their children I wonder where we as a country are headed. We as parents are supposed to protect our children from hurt, harm or danger, but it seems that we are doing just the opposite. We run to our jobs, spending less and less time with our children. We do not talk to our children to gain an understanding of who they are and who they are becoming.

Those first years of our children's lives are the most crucial to their upbringing. It is when they learn right from wrong, what they can do, what they shouldn't do, and what they should do. One person who is up to the task of helping our children be prepared to enter into school and learn the basics of childhood is this young entrepreneur.

Although I may be a little biased in my thinking, I believe that she is one of the most caring, warm hearted, and lover of children that I know. I have seen her grow from a little girl to a great young lady, and now a beautiful woman. I can say that because she is my sister. She is the HART and soul of her family, and the HART and soul of **HEART TWO HART DAYCARE**, meet my baby sister TOUSSANT HART, aka "TUDDY".

BEGINNINGS

Growing up in a small townhouse on the North West side of Baltimore city is where this young entrepreneur got her start. Being the youngest of three children to her mother, she was always looking to pave her own path in life. She would not be coerced into following in the footsteps of her older sister and brother. What this young entrepreneur would do is find her own voice in a household that was full of potential.

Ms. Hart attended elementary and middle school at a seventh day Adventist school (Christian based) and then would go on to attend Northern High school. Our mother wanted to make sure that we got the best education that was available so she made sure that we attended one of the best parochial schools that the seventh day Adventist church had to offer. It did not hurt that we attended the church and she received a discount for us attending the school.

Toussant and I talked about how important we thought that it was that we attended both private and public school. This gave all three of us a firm foundation and a good balance of what to expect in the real world. When a child is sheltered in there up bringing it can lead to their rebellion and out right defiance when they get older.

I know that there are some children who grew up totally sheltered by their parents while growing up and once they entered the "real" world they just went buck wild. The foundation that our mother gave to us has stuck with us to this very day. We may have strayed, as many children do, but all of us have our feet firmly planted in the Lord. We also talked about the sacrifices that our mother made for us so that we could attend the school that we attended.

Our mother has worked two jobs ever since we were little. She made sure that she had a secure job working for the government so that we would always have healthcare and other benefits that a child needs. We now see the benefits of having healthcare and other benefits in a day and time where there are so many people who are doing without it. They are doing without not by choice but by force. People have been forced to go without healthcare because they cannot afford to pay for it. They need every piece of their income to pay for just every day living and there is just not enough left over to have major health care.

Many people are hoping and praying that not having healthcare will not catch up with them. For those who have had mishaps and have had to go to the doctor for whatever reason are now stuck with these enormous medical bills that have left them in debt and with bad credit. I am so glad that my mother was able to give us the safety and security to know if something did happen to us then we were covered. Toussant graduated from

Northern High school and attended Baltimore City Community College (BCCC).

She majored in nursing when she first entered BCCC and would be apart of the BCCC/Coppin State University connect program. She attended BCCC for three years in school before she stopped attending school due to her daughter Kiona being born. She sat out a semester and then went back the following year to continue her education. When she returned to BCCC she changed her major to early childhood education, and attended school for another year before she would see the need for increasing her income to better take care of her family. She says that she changed her major to early childhood education because of her love for children. She has a real soft space in her heart for the nurturing of children, which is what would lead her to starting her own daycare center. While attending school and after she left school, she worked two jobs so that she would be able to make ends meet. She got a strong work ethic from her mother, who taught both of us the value of working hard.

Ms. Hart worked for Right Aide, MCI, BJ's, and Quality Physical Therapy, which was our older sister Larissa's company. As she would do her stint with these jobs, she gained much valued experience about running her own business. While working for Quality Physical Therapy, Ms. Hart would do what was called informal daycare, which is where you do not have your license as a daycare provider.

She says that being in daycare put her into the realm of dealing with children, which is what she wanted to do and it would lead her in the direction of her own business. She says that she really began to focus on having her own business when she would have her third child Derrick Hart Jr. Derrick was born premature and we all were not sure if he would make it. Toussant would spend countless hours even after he was released from the hospital back and forth to the hospital for his care. She says that "with Derrick Jr. needing the care that he needed I wanted to be the one to take care of him and not leave that to someone else". She says that while she was taking care of Derrick she had two other children that she cared for and took the required courses to become a licensed daycare provider. Let this be a lesson to those young people who want to be entrepreneurs, sometimes the path to entrepreneurship is not a direct one and it is certainly not an easy one but if you are focused, committed, and disciplined you will get there.

Being the one to take care of her son was the only option that Ms. Hart would consider and she said that it gave her the push that she needed in order to go for it and start her own business. As she would begin her trek into entrepreneurship she would see the benefits of being able to run and business and be at home. Ms. Hart would run her daycare out of her home, which allowed her the luxury of being able to spend the time that she wanted to with her children and also work and have a successful business.

Many small home businesses allow the business owners to spend quality time with their kids and family and generate income. Many people today are finding their way to run home-based businesses. They are choosing family over the regular 9 to 5 working career. In this day and time it is even more important that we spend quality time with our children.

Children of today have less supervision and less accountability than ever before. They are not learning the values and morals that we learned when we grew up. The more time that we are able to spend at home the more we know what is going on with our children. When we were younger we thought that our parents were just being nosey but I now have come to realize that they are not being nosey they are being protective. The job of a parent is to protect a child. They are to protect that child from the things and people in life that can harm us.

All of us when we were growing up thought that our parents were being mean when they told us that we could not go certain places and could not hang out with certain people. They did this because they did not want to see anything happen to us. As I have gotten older I have come to realize that I do not want to put myself in the position where something bad could happen to me. Yes, there are things that we do not have control over but I believe that if you don't go to certain places or hang with certain people then certain things will not happen to you.

You will find yourself not having to deal with some of the issues that other people have to deal with. One thing that Ms. Hart has stressed with Heart Two Hart Daycare is creating an environment that parents do not have to worry about certain things happening to their children while they are in her care.

THE INDUSTRY

While we have talked about the daycare industry in a previous chapter I would like to look at it from a different perspective. My pastor has the unique ability to take a familiar passage and look at it from different a different perspective. This is what I will attempt to do in this particular segment of this chapter. When it comes to the daycare industry there are daycare providers who will do just the bare minimum that is necessary with the children that they provide for.

At Heart Two Hart they seek to exceed the expectations of their clients. Ms. Hart says that she caters to her parents because she wants them to keep coming back. Each parent has a contract that they must sign, which maps out what the Heart Two Hart Daycare will do for the children. Now with Heart Two Hart Daycare, just as with any other business you want to keep your clients happy and satisfied. The best way to do that is to exceed what they expect from you. Ms. Hart gave an example of a parent who requested that her child begin or complete her homework before she picked her up.

Now this was not in the contract so it was something that Ms. Hart did not have to do. Because she wanted to exceed the expectations of this parent, she made sure that this child either started her homework or completed it as the parent had requested. When you go beyond the expectations of your clients, they will come back to you again and again.

Ms. Hart says that if her parents want to come in and have a conversation with her than she will do that, "it's all about catering to your client". Ms. Hart says that her daycare children are just like her own. She says that she listens to them, she encourages them, she gives them hugs and she communicates with them. She says that when you talk with children they give you a lot of information, whether it is solicited or unsolicited. Children can be a wealth of information. They will tell you things that will blow you away sometimes. What Ms. Hart and the Heart Two Hart Daycare family do is allow children to be children without any inhibitions. Children need to be allowed to grow up and be children along the way to adulthood.

They want to be able to rip and run, eat, and enjoy life and that is what Heart Two Hart allows them to do. Ms. Hart also likes to impart the learning process with her kids. She makes sure that her children are well prepared to enter school. Ms. Hart takes her children on trips that will teach the children something as well as have some fun along the way. Whether it is the amusement park or the library the Heart Two Hart Daycare will make sure that the children have a smooth transition from infancy to kindergarten.

It is amazing what you can learn about your siblings when you sit and talk with them. Doing this profile of my sister has taught me the strong business mind that each of us has developed. In the daycare industry just as any other industry, the name of the game is "DIVERSITY". Just as any stockowner, or business owner will tell you the larger your portfolio the better your bottom-line. Ms. Hart is no different from any other business owner who has seen the value in diversifying her portfolio. She says that in her industry you can set your own income range according to how much money you want to bring in. She says that she takes kids before school, after school and kids that are with her all day.

She says that she is able to set her income based on what she charges. She also talked about if she wants to increase the amount of income that she has for a certain month, she will use referrals from other daycare providers. She gave an example that during the Christmas season she may want to make some extra money so she knows that some daycare providers like to take vacations during that time so she will watch their children during that time for them. This is a very creative way to increase her bottom line and at the same time help parents out, it is a win/win situation.

Ms. Hart also adds a different dynamic to her business in running a carpool through her daycare. She has children that she takes to school in the morning and then she picks them up in the afternoon. She is able to offer this service, which is not a service that a lot of other daycare providers offer. Ms. Hart has found multiple ways to stand out from the rest of the daycare industry.

With her daycare she has a different learning program for each child. She has a program that her 1 year olds go through, she has a program for 2 year olds, and on up. She says that she wants her children to be prepared when they enter school. She also makes sure that her children are constantly busy; she says that during the summertime she and the kids are always doing something. She says that they do not go as many places during the school year of course but during the summer time they are able to get in the minivan and roll out! Keeping kids active is very important. An idle mind is the devils workshop, and Ms. Hart makes sure that the devil has no room in her children's minds.

Children are a bundle of energy and its good to know that there are individuals such as Ms. Hart who love to channel that energy and gear it in the right direction. When your children enter Heart Two Hart Daycare you know that they will do more than sit around all day watching stories, eating bon bons, and laying around on the couch. Heart Two Hart is not in the business of raising the next Peggy Bundy; they are in the business of raising the next Barack Obama, Oprah Winfrey, or Tyler Perry.

THE FUTURE

Ms. Hart says that her daycare almost did not come to existence. She says that when she was in the beginning stages of starting her business they were in the process of trying to pass a bill that would require home based daycares that were in the basement to have a basement ceiling that was 7' tall. They kept Ms. Hart in limbo because of the delay in this bill trying to be passed. Well, the bill was never passed because of many of the row homes do not have ceilings that were over 7' tall and this is the major reason that the bill was not passed. Since the bill was not passed

Ms. Hart has been able to go full speed ahead and will continue that into the future. Staying focused is the key to moving any business into the future. Ms. Hart believes that you must be honest and focused in order to keep your business headed in the right direction.

Whether it is starting a business or growing a business there is always capital that will be needed. Ms. Hart says that with her business there were certain regulations that she had to meet for her house and other things that she needed for her the children.

She says that the majority of the initial capital that she had to use was straight out of pocket. She says that she also received gifts from those around her for the things that she would need in the daycare, such as toys, cribs, and other gifts to help her get her business off the ground.

Ms. Hart makes sure that her business does not mix with her family life. She says, "when the last child leaves on Friday, I do not go down into the basement until Monday". She says that it is important when you are dealing with a home-based business, especially when you have children all day long you have to have a balance. When you don't have that balance you can create frustration for yourself. Ms. Hart says that she treats her basement, which is where her daycare is, just like her office. When she is gone she is gone!

Ms. Hart says that she is planning on going back to college to get her associates degree and go on to get her masters in early childhood education. Ms. Hart says that she also wants to open a group home and also have a daycare center, to help our youth of today. She believes that so many of our youth are misguided and she wants to help them head in the right direction. Being able to offer our youth a positive alternative to the negative draws of the streets of today, is what Ms. Hart wants to be able to give to her community. She wants to make a difference, and believes that she has a lot to offer in this world that is full of negativity for our youth. I believe that this strong, nurturing, intelligent, and progressive young entrepreneur will have no problem moving herself as well as Hart 2 Hart Daycare into the future.

When I look at this young entrepreneur and I see how she has grown into this great businesswoman and a great woman in general, I can't help but think about us growing up in that townhouse on the Northwest side of Baltimore and then to the Northeast side of Baltimore and I say that we have come a long way from playing nurf basketball in between the living room and dining room of our home. I love you Toussant and I am proud to call myself your brother!

REFLECTIONS

Wow!!! That is all that I can say about this project. This has been some journey that I have been apart of. I cannot put into words the heart felt gratitude that I have for the men and women who have blessed me by being apart of this project/book. It is amazing to me to look back over this body of work and to see how it has developed into something that I am very proud of. When I started my company my aim was to enlighten, empower, and to invest in the lives that would support my business.

I have been taught that we are blessed to bless and the Lord has truly blessed me and I hope that I am able to bless someone else with what he has given to me. This project has enlightened, empowered, and invested in my life personally. This book has taken me to places that I did not know that I could go myself. What we all must do in life is to continue to progress. This book has helped me to progress as a Christian, as an individual, and as an entrepreneur.

As I think of the many images that are given to us on television, in the newspaper, and on the radio, I hope that I was able to bring to you a different way of looking at men and women of color. Change begins in the mind. When a persons mind is renewed then they begin to make better decisions. When we make better decisions then we alleviate many of the stresses that come our way.

The way that we change our surroundings is by educating people on the choices that they have. I believe that when people have access to resources they can thrive and be successful. Our world is changing and we as black people have to understand that change if we are going to be a part of it. We have more opportunities than we have had in the past and we have more resources than we have had as well. We must see ourselves elevated and lifted up. We cannot be afraid to give back what has been given to us. They say that to whom much is given much is required. We need to start requiring more of ourselves. We must begin to start and hold each other accountable for our actions. We can no longer accept mediocrity as our standard. We must constantly be striving to be **EXTRA-ORDINARY** in everything that we do.

We must believe that we can excel in every aspect of life. We are great businessmen and women who have a voice in this society. We must take our rightful place and let everyone know that we are achievers!!! In the pages of this book are individuals who dared to not only have a vision but they took on the challenge of bringing those visions to reality. The path to entrepreneurship is not the same for everyone, but the final destination is the same. I think of Malcolm X and Martin Luther King Jr. and the journey that each of them walked. The final destination for each of them was to set a people free, but the means for each of them to accomplish that freedom was not the same. The entrepreneurs that you have read about in this book have all taken different paths to get to own there own business but the end result is that they are business owners. They are people who have wanted to make a difference in someone else's life and leave this world better off then when they came into it.

Some of these entrepreneurs I knew personally and some I knew about, and others I did not know at all, but what I have gotten after this project is a group of individuals who have chosen to share with me apart of themselves and I in turn have shared it with you. I have some old friends that are in this book and I hope to have made some new ones as well. I want to personally thank each and every entrepreneur who believed enough in me to want to be a part of this project. I hope that this book has helped someone to see that we can do and will continue to do great things!!! I thank my Lord and Savior Jesus Christ for the gift that he has given me and I will continue to use it to Change lives and Save Souls!!!!

JNF ENTERPRISES BOOK ORDER FORM

Ship Book To:

Name: _____

Address:

_____

_____

Email Address:

_____

Title of Book: _____

Quantity___Cost:_____

Mail order form and to request directory of Entrepreneurs Contact:

JNF Enterprises

8813 StoneRidge Circle

#103

Pikesville, MD 21208

For Money orders: Please allow 7-10 days for delivery; for personal checks, please allow 14-21 days for delivery as we have to wait for the check to clear.

Checks should be made out to: JNF Enterprises c/o Leroy C. McKenzie Jr.

A receipt will be mailed when we receive your payment.

JNF thanks you for your Support!!

Leroy C. McKenzie Jr.

ABOUT THE AUTHOR

Leroy C. Mckenzie Jr. is the author of "The Customer Is Not Always Right, A Common Sense Guide To Establishing a Strong and Flourishing Business". He resides in Baltimore, Maryland. He is a Devout Christian, Poet, and Entrepreneur. He is at work on his fifth project.

Ms. Vickie Stringer
TCP Publications

Ms. Joi Thomas
Joiful Communications

Ms. Tynese Daniels
Elite-Physiquues

Ms. Harrine Freeman
H.E. Freeman Enterprises

Mr. Brian Howard
Howard Residential Srv.

Ms. Lisa Ennis
Eccentrics-
The Spa Sanctuary

Ms. Jerronda Davis
Liberty Consulting Srv.

Mr. Melvin Lowe, Jr.
Designs by JR/Defining Moments

Ms. Ghilda Williams-Cole
Sole Proprietor
Long & Foster

Ms. Jennene Biggins
Voluptuous Woman Co.

Mr. Scott Newell
Tires On The Go, Inc.

Mr. Allan Taylor
Taylor Made Transportation

Ms. Monique Lemmon
Joyful Noice Day Care

Mr. Max Fortune
The Platinum Agency

Mr. Ernest Burley
Burley Insurance &
Financial Srv.

Ms. Sandra Pearsall
Real Estate Investor

Ms. Julie Williamson
A Good Book Bookstore

Mr. Farrajii Muhammad
New Light
Leadership Coalition, Inc.

Ms. Lorenz Robinson Reese
Simply Savvy Events, LLC.

Ms. Kimberly Thomas, Esq.
The Law Offices of
Kimberly M. Thomas

Ms. Toussant Hart
Heart Two Hart Day Care